HIV for non-HIV specialists

Diagnosing the undiagnosed

A practical guide for healthcare professionals in
secondary care to support improved detection and
diagnosis of HIV in the UK

By Dr Rachel Baggaley

MEDICAL FOUNDATION FOR AIDS
& SEXUAL HEALTH (MedFASH)

A charity supported by the British Medical Association

Registered charity no: 296689

Acknowledgements

MedFASH is grateful for advice and assistance from a wide range of individuals and organisations during the development of this booklet. Particular thanks go to the project advisory group:

Dr Mary Armitage, Dr Nick Beeching, Dr Christine Blanshard, Dr Gary Brook, Dr Jose Catalan, Dr Susie Forster, Professor Margaret Johnson, Peter Keogh, Dr Nick Levell, Professor Rob Miller, Angelina Namiba, Charles Oduka, Kay Orton (for the Department of Health), Dr Angela Robinson, Jack Summerside, Dr Sarah Whitfield, Heather Wilson.

Special thanks are due to Dr Hermione Lyall who wrote Section 3.12 on paediatric HIV.

Thanks also to Yusef Azad, Tracy Barnes, Dr Ed Beveridge, Pete Boyle, Christine Cavanagh, Genevieve Clark, Dr Darren Cousins, Maggie Duckett, Amanda Evans, Dr Martin Fisher, Vicky Gilbart, Andrew Gilliver, Professor Ian Gilmore, Phil Greenham, Dr Ian Hodgson, Richard Jones, Professor George Kinghorn, Marion Lerwin, Professor Sue Lightman, Dr Hermione Lyall, Dr Sara Madge, Dr Hadi Manji, Brenda Mann, Carmelo di Maria, Wendy Martin, Dr Philippa Matthews, Ed McConniffe, Dr Lesley Navaratne, Dr Mark Nelson, Dr Ed Ong, Lois Orton, Melanie Ottewill, Dr Adrian Palfreeman, Jason Penn, Nathan Perry, Elias Phiri, Jonathan Roberts, Dr Surinder Singh, Jane Stokes, Dr Nick Theobald, Sarah Zetler.

The UK National Guidelines for HIV Testing 2008 prepared jointly by British Association for Sexual Health and HIV (BASHH), British HIV Association (BHIVA) and British Infection Society (BIS) – copyright BHIVA 2008, reproduced with permission.

The development, printing and dissemination of this booklet have been funded by the Department of Health.

Project management and editing, Russell Fleet, MedFASH Project Manager.
Project administration, Magnus Nelson, MedFASH Administrator.
Design and layout by Hilary Tranter.
MedFASH Executive Director, Ruth Lowbury.

Published by

Medical Foundation for AIDS & Sexual Health
BMA House, Tavistock Square, WC1H 9JP

Cover:
HIV particles. Chris Bjornberg/Science Photo Library

ISBN number: 978-0-9549973-3-5

© Medical Foundation for AIDS & Sexual Health (MedFASH) 2008

CONTENTS

CONTENTS

Followed by: The British Association for Sexual Health and HIV (BASHH), British HIV Association (BHIVA) and British Infection Society (BIS)
UK National Guidelines for HIV Testing 2008

Foreword

Much has changed in the field of HIV in the UK. A diagnosis of HIV used to be considered a death sentence, but over the past decade there have been major advances in the management of HIV-related conditions.

r Mary Armitage

Care by a specialist team, including the use of antiretroviral therapy, has transformed the outlook for many patients, for most of whom HIV may now be considered a chronic disease. However, early diagnosis and management contribute substantially to this improvement in prognosis whereas those who are diagnosed late have greatly increased morbidity and mortality.

It has been estimated that over 73,000 people have HIV in the UK, yet nearly a third of these are undiagnosed. Over the past five years there have been more than 7,000 new diagnoses per year, and around one third are late. Furthermore, delayed diagnosis accounts for at least 35 per cent of HIV-related deaths. Early diagnosis reduces the risk of onward transmission, both because effective treatment itself reduces infectiousness and because diagnosis allows modification of behaviour to reduce the risk.

Yet many patients who are diagnosed late have been seen previously in other parts of the healthcare system. Opportunities to make an earlier diagnosis were missed. Why are we failing to diagnose HIV, and how can we improve the care that patients should be receiving? It is true that HIV is not always easy to diagnose – many of the symptoms are vague or non-specific. Patients with HIV-related symptoms and signs can present in any secondary care setting and to a range of non-HIV specialists who may not see many cases and have a low index of suspicion. These difficulties are compounded by the historical perception that HIV testing is different, difficult and not part of routine testing when considering differential diagnoses. Clinicians may feel reluctant to raise the possibility of what is still seen as a stigmatising diagnosis, and they may have concerns about exceptional requirements for secrecy. They may find it difficult to initiate the discussion, or believe that special counselling skills are required.

FOREWORD

In 2007, a letter from the Chief Medical and Nursing Officers highlighted the importance of improving the detection and diagnosis of HIV. The Department of Health has funded a range of activities to increase the rates of diagnosis and to de-stigmatise HIV, and this booklet from the Medical Foundation for AIDS & Sexual Health (MedFASH) is part of the strategy. During my term as Clinical Vice President of the Royal College of Physicians, I had the opportunity to work collaboratively with BHIVA, BASHH and BIS, resulting in establishing standards for HIV services, and I was delighted to be invited by MedFASH to chair the Advisory Group to develop guidance for non-HIV specialists.

We wanted to produce practical help and advice to raise awareness amongst non-HIV specialists, to reduce barriers to testing and to ensure that HIV testing becomes routine. The booklet provides an overview of the many common presenting conditions when generalists should consider a diagnosis of HIV and strategies for approaching the offer of an HIV test. We were fortunate that our project coincided with the production of updated guidelines for carrying out HIV testing in all healthcare settings, led jointly by BHIVA, BASHH and BIS. We have worked together to ensure that the two pieces of work complement and support each other.

I would like to thank the members of the Advisory Group who have given so much time and expertise, and also Russell and Ruth from MedFASH for their enthusiasm and hard work in support of the project. Our aims are to reduce levels of undiagnosed HIV and to increase earlier diagnoses, and we hope that this booklet will help to achieve these outcomes.

Dr Mary Armitage BSc, MBChB (hons), DM, FRCP, FRCPE,
Immediate Past Clinical Vice-President, Royal College of Physicians.

Preface

About this booklet
This booklet is one in a series of practical tools to explain the rationale and promote the need for increased HIV testing in all clinical settings to help reduce the level of undiagnosed HIV infection in the UK, and to improve communication about patients with HIV between health professionals who share their care. It is based on the successful MedFASH booklet, HIV in Primary Care, by Dr Sara Madge, Dr Philippa Matthews, Dr Surinder Singh and Dr Nick Theobald.

It is designed to complement the *UK National Guidelines for HIV Testing 2008* published by the British Association for Sexual Health and HIV (BASHH), British HIV Association (BHIVA) and the British Infection Society (BIS). It should be noted that the guidelines are intended for practitioners in all healthcare settings and therefore some of the recommendations in them are more applicable to primary care than secondary care. For information about HIV diagnosis and testing in primary care, please refer to Madge et al mentioned above.

The focus of this booklet is on HIV testing and diagnosis and it is aimed specifically at non-HIV specialist clinicians working in secondary care settings who are likely to encounter undiagnosed HIV in patients either in specialist outpatient clinics, or who are admitted to hospital as inpatients to general medical wards via their GP or via the emergency department. The booklet provides supplementary information to that given in the guidelines, as well as case studies and concrete strategies to assist non-HIV specialist clinicians in detecting undiagnosed HIV and implementing HIV testing in their daily practice. For ease of use the guidelines are reprinted in their entirety at the back of this booklet.

About the author
Dr Rachel Baggaley is Head of HIV at Christian Aid, a UK based development agency which supports more than 250 HIV projects in 40 developing countries. She is also an honorary research fellow at the London School of Hygiene and Tropical Medicine and works one day a week in a clinic in South London. Previously she spent six years working on HIV programmes in Zambia and then for the World Health Organization in Geneva on guidelines for antiretroviral therapy in developing countries, HIV testing and counselling and the prevention of mother-to-child transmission.

About the Medical Foundation for AIDS & Sexual Health (MedFASH)

MedFASH is a charity supported by the British Medical Association. It works with policy-makers and health professionals to promote excellence in the prevention and management of HIV and other sexually transmitted infections. Recent work includes a review of GUM services in England, managing the development of the Royal College of General Practitioners' Introductory Certificate in Sexual Health and undertaking a review of the *National strategy for sexual health and HIV* for the Independent Advisory Group on Sexual Health and HIV.

Comments about this booklet are welcome, and will inform future editions. Please send them to the Medical Foundation for AIDS & Sexual Health.

Whilst all reasonable efforts have been made to ensure the information contained in this booklet is accurate, no representations or warranties are made (whether expressed or implied) as to the reliability or completeness of such information. Neither the Medical Foundation for AIDS & Sexual Health nor the author can be held liable for any consequence or loss arising directly or indirectly from the use of, or any action taken in reliance on, any information appearing in this booklet.

SECTION 1

HIV in the UK:
an overview

HIV in the UK:
an overview

Background

Human immunodeficiency virus (HIV) is one of the most important communicable diseases in the UK. There were an estimated 73,000 people living with HIV infection in the UK at the end of 2006[1]. Annual numbers of new HIV diagnoses in the UK more than doubled between 1997 and 2003 (from 2,768 to 7,350), and have increased more slowly since then to reach a peak of 7,734 in 2007[2].

There has been effective treatment for HIV since the mid 1990s. Antiretroviral therapy (ART) and other interventions have resulted in a dramatic reduction in the number of HIV-related deaths in the UK, and most infected people in the UK are living with HIV as a chronic condition rather than an inevitably fatal illness.

Over the past decade there has been a rapid increase in the number c HIV infections diagnosed in the UK which were acquired throug

Figure 1: First HIV and AIDS diagnoses in the UK, and deaths among HIV infected individuals 1998 to 2007

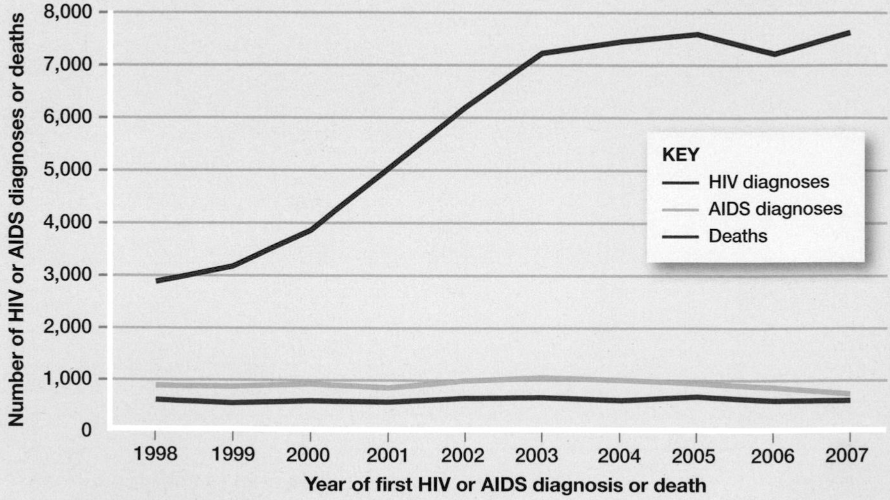

KEY
— HIV diagnoses
— AIDS diagnoses
— Deaths

Source: Health Protection Agency Centre for Infections. Data to end June, 2008.

HIV FOR NON-HIV SPECIALIST

heterosexual sex (see figure 2), and these account for just over half of all new diagnoses annually. Of these, the majority were acquired abroad, mostly attributable to exposure in sub-Saharan Africa. African-born men and women made up 35 per cent of all adults with HIV in the UK in 2006, and accounted for 68 per cent of all heterosexually acquired infections.

There are still high levels of HIV transmission in men who have sex with men (MSM) and since 2001 the number of HIV diagnoses reported annually has consistently exceeded the annual number of diagnoses throughout the 1990s. It is believed that 83 per cent of these men acquired their infection in the UK.

Undiagnosed HIV
It is believed that at the end of 2006 about 21,600 HIV-infected people aged 15-59 remained undiagnosed in the UK, approximately a third of the total infected[1]. Of these undiagnosed adults, 43 per cent were estimated to be men who have sex with men (MSM), 51 per cent heterosexuals (mostly African-born), and 5 per cent injecting drug users.

Late diagnosis
HIV-related morbidity and mortality are increasingly concentrated among those who are diagnosed late. Although many of these patients will do well, some will be left with permanent disability and many will take longer

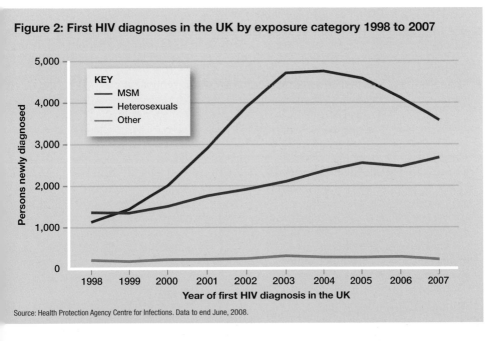

Figure 2: First HIV diagnoses in the UK by exposure category 1998 to 2007

KEY
— MSM
— Heterosexuals
— Other

Persons newly diagnosed

Year of first HIV diagnosis in the UK

Source: Health Protection Agency Centre for Infections. Data to end June, 2008.

to respond well to treatment[3]. Early diagnosis is also more cost-effective as timely initiation of ART leads to fewer episodes of acute serious illness[4]

A recent audit of deaths caused by HIV among adults reported that in approximately 25 per cent of cases diagnosis occurred too late for optimal treatment (and that late diagnosis accounted for 35 per cent of HIV-related deaths)[5]. This highlights the need to improve diagnosis of HIV by increasing the uptake of HIV testing. There is also evidence that a significant proportion of people who are diagnosed late with HIV have been seen by healthcare professionals at some point in the year previous to diagnosis with what were, in retrospect, HIV-associated symptoms but were not offered an HIV test[6].

The Health Protection Agency (HPA) currently defines late diagnosis as having a CD4 cell count at diagnosis of less than 200 cells/mm[3]. However if late diagnosis is defined as having a CD4 count less than 350 cells/mm (ie below the threshold currently recommended for starting ART) this figure rises to 57 per cent.

see page 14 for the CD4 count

In late 2007 the UK's four Chief Medical Officers (CMOs) and Chief Nursing Officers (CNOs) wrote to all doctors and nurses setting out good practice to improve the detection and diagnosis of HIV in non-HIV specialist settings and reminding them of the need to consider offering an HIV test, where clinically indicated[7,8,9,10]. This is in line with international recommendations from the World Health Organization (WHO)[11]. In the USA the Centers for Disease Control and Prevention (CDC)[12] have recommended that screening for HIV infection should be performed routinely for all patients aged 13-64 years in all healthcare settings. Because the UK's overall HIV prevalence is approximately 0.1 per cent it is unlikely that routine screening of the whole population on the US model will be adopted on grounds of cost-effectiveness as HIV in the UK is concentrated in distinct population sub-groups.

Many clinicians believe that discussing HIV with patients is difficult, or that patients need 'pre-test counselling' by a trained counsellor. This is not the case and this was highlighted by the UK CMOs' Expert Advisory Group on AIDS as long ago as 1996 in guidelines on pre-test discussion for HIV testing[13]. This cautious approach to offering an HIV test is a legacy of a time when the prognosis for those infected with HIV was poor and treatment options were limited. Since the mid-1990s, ART has transformed long-term health outcomes for people with HIV, although no cure is as yet available.

However, HIV remains a highly stigmatised health condition in the UK

The case for earlier diagnosis

57 per cent of people with HIV in the UK are diagnosed at a late stage.
This results in:
- a worse prognosis with significantly increased risk of permanent disability
- a significant increase in mortality
- ongoing transmission to sexual partners.

Most people diagnosed late will have had prior contact with healthcare workers.

The case for routine HIV testing

- HIV testing should be seen as a normal part of the diagnostic process and a duty of care
- Where routine HIV testing is in place, uptake of testing is increased
- The exceptional approach to HIV testing has been a barrier to clinicians in offering testing and to patients in accessing it
- 'Normalising' HIV testing will help to reduce stigma
- Failure to diagnose HIV leads to avoidable deaths and serious illness
- Effective HIV treatment reduces infectiousness and can reduce onward transmission

and this often deters people from actively seeking a test, as well as deterring clinicians from offering one. While there are clear individual and public health[14,15] benefits to offering HIV testing, and it should be offered and recommended to everyone who could have been exposed to HIV infection, clinicians need to be aware that patients may have reservations about being tested for HIV and these are discussed later in the booklet.

The natural history of HIV infection

HIV is a retrovirus which preferentially infects immune system cells, particularly the CD4 lymphocytes. It is present in an infected person's blood, and is also present in other body fluids, such as semen, vaginal secretions, rectal secretions and breast milk.

The 'window' period

Antibodies to HIV typically appear between four to six weeks after infection, but this may take as long as 12 weeks. This is commonly referred to as the 'window' period. During this period an HIV antibody test will not detect the infection but the virus is still present. The p24 antigen is a protein of the virus itself and can be detected in a blood sample for a short period after infection (normally from two to five weeks). However, it rapidly becomes undetectable once antibodies to HIV start to develop. It is therefore useful in identifying early HIV infection but not for established infection.

Primary HIV infection or seroconversion

see page 44 in section 3.11 for signs of primary HIV infection

The patient may experience a flu-like illness at the time of infection. Symptoms develop in over 60 per cent of people at this stage. They may be mild and non-specific, but they can also be marked and precipitate a referral to secondary care or a visit to the emergency department.

Stages of HIV infection

Asymptomatic stage

Once the symptoms of primary HIV infection subside, the asymptomatic stage of the infection begins. There are usually no overt clinical signs and symptoms of HIV infection during this stage and the individual with HIV may be well for some or many years with a CD4 count of over 500 cells/mm^3. Some laboratory tests may be abnormal, eg anaemia, neutropenia, lymphopenia, thrombocytopenia, and diffuse hypergammaglobulinaemia.

The CD4 count declines at a rate of approximately 40-80 cells/mm^3 per year in untreated individuals, but some progress faster than others. There is wide variation in the time it takes to progress from primary infection to symptomatic disease (see figure 3).

Symptomatic stage

If untreated, infection with HIV results in the development of HIV-associated or opportunistic infections (OIs). Fungi, viruses, bacteria and other organisms that are usually harmless can all cause OIs. Some, eg candidiasis (oral and/or vaginal), are more common in the immunocompromised. Others, eg Pneumocystis pneumonia (PCP) only cause infection in the immunocompromised.

Constitutional symptoms may occur. These include fevers, night sweats, headache, malaise, fatigue, diarrhoea and weight loss. Generalised lymphadenopathy involving extra-inguinal sites may be present.

Other conditions may occur including oral hairy leukoplakia, shingles, recurrent herpes simplex outbreaks and episodes of seborrhoeic dermatitis, folliculitis and psoriasis.

Bacterial infections (most commonly *Streptococcus pneumoniae*, *Haemophilus influenzae* and *Staphylococcus aureus*) may occur during this stage, leading to sinusitis, bronchitis and pneumonia.

Symptomatic (AIDS-defining)

Some infections and malignancies are associated with HIV infection and their diagnosis classifies an HIV-infected patient as having developed AIDS. Other conditions including neurological disease associated with HIV and excessive weight loss (more than 10kg) may also lead to an AIDS diagnosis.

Later stages of infection are associated with infections including PCP, cytomegalovirus (CMV), progressive multifocal leucoencephalopathy (PML), *Mycobacterium avium-intracellulare* (MAI), cryptococcosis, cryptosporidiosis, toxoplasma encephalitis, and oesophageal candidiasis. Individuals are also at increased risk of malignancies including Kaposi's sarcoma (KS), non-Hodgkin's lymphoma and malignancies of the cervix and anus associated with human papilloma virus (HPV).

Diagnostic markers

CD4 count

see page 20 for the different HIV tests

The CD4 lymphocyte count is a useful indicator of the degree of immunosuppression in those infected with HIV. In healthy, non-HIV-infected individuals the CD4 count is usually above 500 cells/mm^3, although some individuals have naturally lower CD4 counts. It is normal for CD4 counts to be variable. Trends are therefore more important than single readings. Patients with a CD4 count of below 200 cells/mm^3 are at risk of HIV-related opportunistic infections and tumours, but some may not have significant symptoms.

The CD4 count is a valuable clinical tool in deciding when to start antiretroviral therapy (ART) and when to commence prophylaxis against opportunistic infections.

Viral load

This is a measure of the amount of HIV in the blood. Viral load can range from undetectable to over a million copies/ml.

The degree of viral replication is linked to the rate of CD4 decline, and hence disease progression. The aim of ART is to reduce viral load to undetectable levels. A rising viral load in a patient on ART can indicate a range of problems, eg drug resistance may be developing or the patient may not be adhering to their treatment regimen.

How the CD4 count and viral load interrelate

If HIV is replicating at high levels the viral load predicts a more rapid CD4 decline. The CD4 count of patients not taking ART who have a high viral load is likely to fall more rapidly than that of those with a lower viral load. Once the viral load is suppressed CD4 counts recover with a decreased risk of developing OIs, tumours and other complications of HIV infection (see figure 3).

Figure 3. Association between virological, immunological, and clinical events and time course of HIV infection

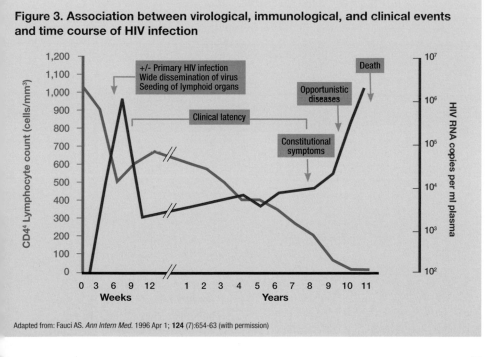

Adapted from: Fauci AS. *Ann Intern Med.* 1996 Apr 1; **124** (7):654-63 (with permission)

SECTION 2

Recommendations for testing

Recommendations for testing

Who can perform an HIV test?

People with undiagnosed HIV may potentially be seen in any hospital outpatient clinic or ward, and offering HIV testing to patients should be considered during any clinical contact. With forethought and preparation, it is within the competence of all clinicians and appropriately trained healthcare workers to obtain consent for and perform an HIV test. There is no need for special counselling skills beyond those required for routine clinical practice.

Who should be recommended an HIV test?

HIV testing has historically been managed on an 'opt-in' basis, ie levels of uptake have been determined by patients actively coming forward for testing. However, the positive experience of offering HIV testing as routine to all patients attending antenatal services and in larger urban areas to all patients attending GUM services, demonstrates that offering HIV testing on an 'opt-out' basis, ie as a routine investigation, increases the likelihood of patients agreeing to test.

The *UK National Guidelines for HIV Testing 2008* from BASHH, BHIVA and BIS recommend that HIV testing is made routine under the following circumstances.

Routine HIV testing for all people attending specific services

It is recognised that with some clinical services there is a potentially increased HIV prevalence amongst attendees and compelling reasons exist to identify HIV early. Such services include:

GUM or sexual health clinics. Risk factors for sexually transmitted infections are the same as those for HIV infection and in GUM settings it is standard policy to include an HIV test routinely within the full sexual health screen.

Antenatal services. Since the introduction of the universal recommendation of antenatal HIV testing in the UK in 1998, the mother-to-child transmission rate has remained below 2 per cent[16].

Termination of pregnancy services. There is evidence from unlinked anonymous seroprevalence surveys conducted in inner London termination clinics that there is a higher prevalence of HIV infection in women terminating their pregnancies compared with those giving birth.

Drug dependency programmes. Injecting drug use is a recognised risk factor for HIV infection and undiagnosed HIV prevalence among injecting drug users was 39 per cent at the end of 2006[1].

Services for patients with tuberculosis, hepatitis B/C and lymphoma. There is an increased risk of HIV infection in patients with these conditions. Treatment for these conditions may therefore have to be changed for patients in these groups.

Dialysis, blood donation and organ transplant services. Patients with chronic kidney disease (CKD) are routinely screened for HIV infection before initiation of dialysis[17]. It is standard practice to test anyone who is being put forward for a transplant for HIV, as it is for anyone donating blood or tissues/organs.

Other services not mentioned in the guidelines, but where routine HIV testing of all patients would be good practice are:

Services for patients requiring immunosuppressant therapy. Immunosuppressant therapy in a patient already immunocompromised by undiagnosed HIV risks unforeseen complications[18].

Haemophilia services. In the UK blood for transfusion has been screened and blood products heat-treated for HIV since the mid 1980's, but patients who have received treatment from countries where screening procedures are not in place should be offered HIV testing.

Services for victims of rape. The acute situation should be managed by specialist services. All victims of rape should be offered full screening for STIs including HIV and offered post-exposure prophylaxis (PEP) if appropriate.

see page 73 for PEP and exposure incidents

Services for people who have occupational exposure to blood or blood products. All healthcare settings should have clear guidelines, referral and support procedures for this eventuality as detailed in the DH guidelines on post-exposure prophylaxis (PEP) following occupational exposure[19].

Services for people requesting post-exposure prophylaxis following sexual exposure (PEPSE). The BASHH guideline for the use of PEPSE stipulates that it is mandatory to test individuals for whom PEPSE is provided, using a test with rapid result, prior to or shortly after commencing therapy to prevent inadvertent and unplanned treatment of pre-existing undiagnosed HIV infection[20].

Routine HIV testing for all people who present for healthcare where HIV enters the differential diagnosis

Some conditions, eg Kaposi's sarcoma and CMV retinitis, are highly associated with HIV infection and their presence should prompt HIV testing. Other conditions indicating a need for HIV testing include tuberculosis, hepatitis B/C and lymphoma.

Many of the problems associated with HIV are also observed in people without HIV infection, eg seborrhoeic dermatitis, herpes zoster and folliculitis. However, these are more common in the HIV-infected and they are more likely to be recurrent or slow to resolve. It is therefore recommended that HIV should enter the differential diagnosis in these instances and testing should be performed.

SECTION 2

see page 44 in section 3.11 for signs of primary HIV infection

Glandular fever-like illnesses are associated with HIV seroconversion (primary HIV infection) and should therefore prompt testing.

Routine HIV testing for all people who belong to a group at higher risk of HIV infection

People from populations at higher risk of HIV infection may attend clinical services other than those mentioned above. The *UK National Guidelines for HIV Testing 2008* recommend they be offered an HIV test routinely. Risk should be discussed without pre-judgement. These groups are:
- all individuals diagnosed with a sexually transmitted infection
- all individuals with a current or former sexual partner with HIV
- all men who have sex with men
- all female sexual contacts of men who have sex with men
- all individuals who report a history of injecting drug use
- all individuals from countries of high HIV prevalence*
- all sexual contacts of individuals from countries of high HIV prevalence.*

*A table ranking countries by adult HIV prevalence rates can be found online at http://www.unaids.org/en/KnowledgeCentre/HIVData/Epidemiology/latestEpiData.asp[21].

It is also useful to consider routine HIV testing for the following:
- all individuals with a current or former sexual partner with a history of injecting drug use
- all individuals who have received injections, blood transfusions, blood products, transplants or other risk-prone healthcare-related procedures in countries without rigorous programmes of equipment sterilisation, screening of blood, organs and tissues or treatment of blood products.

Routine HIV testing in areas where the diagnosed HIV prevalence exceeds 2 in 1,000

The US experience of offering universal HIV testing to all people presenting for healthcare aged between 13 and 64 recognises that screening is only cost-effective in areas where the prevalence of undiagnosed HIV exceeds 1 in 1,000[12]. As undiagnosed prevalence in the UK is half that of diagnosed prevalence, the *UK National Guidelines for HIV Testing 2008* recommend offering routine HIV testing to the following patients in an area where diagnosed HIV prevalence in the local population (PCT or Local Authority) exceeds 2 in 1,000:
- all men and women registering in primary care
- all general medical admissions.

Which test to use?
Laboratory testing
The most commonly used test looks for both the HIV-1 and HIV-2 antibody and the HIV p24 antigen. This is an improvement on the previous

20   HIV FOR NON-HIV SPECIALISTS

generation of HIV tests which looked for antibodies only, and can give a reliable result from as little as 28 days after exposure. In the event of a positive result a second sample is requested for confirmation.

HIV RNA quantitative assays are a form of Nucleic Acid Amplification Test (NAAT). These are not often used as an initial diagnostic test for HIV in adults as they are expensive and have a high false positivity rate. However they may be offered in special circumstances, eg following recent potential exposure where post-exposure-prophylaxis is being considered, and are now the preferred test to diagnose early infection if primary HIV infection is suspected and the antibody/antigen test is negative.

Point of care testing

Point of care testing uses rapid testing devices which look for antibodies only, but they have the advantage that a test result can be given within 15 minutes of the specimen being taken and the result can be delivered at the initial consultation. The specificity of rapid testing devices is lower than that of the standard laboratory tests. In low prevalence settings this may result in a significant number of false positive results. It is therefore essential that all positive point of care test results are confirmed with a conventional blood test. The British Association for Sexual Health and HIV (BASHH) has produced a guideline on point of care testing[22] which suggests the use of rapid testing devices may be suitable for:

- GUM clinics
- obstetric settings for high-risk patients
- PCT-run community clinics
- outreach settings
- source patient testing prior to post-exposure prophylaxis (PEP) for both occupational and sexual exposure
- individuals presenting for post-exposure prophylaxis following sexual exposure (PEPSE) to prevent inadvertent and unplanned treatment of pre-existing undiagnosed HIV infection.

Rapid testing devices may also be purchased via internet sites and there are anecdotal reports of people self-testing. People who purchase internet tests may not fully understand their limitations in terms of sensitivity and specificity, and may be unaware of the need to confirm results and the need for re-testing if within the window period.

The national *Standards for HIV Clinical Care* (2007) recommend that all patients who test positive in any setting are booked into a specialist HIV clinic within 14 days of diagnosis to have their results confirmed and for further assessment and management[23].

see page 13 for more on the window period

How often to test?

Because of the time taken for antibodies to appear, repeat testing should be offered as a precaution to anyone who is at risk from recent exposure and is within the 'window' period. Although this can be as little as a month if a fourth generation assay which detects both antibody and antigen is used, the window period is considered to be three months.

Annual testing can be offered to those at high risk from infection such as men who have sex with men (MSM), injecting drug users or sexual partners of people with HIV.

Because of the success of universal antenatal screening, it is recommended to repeat the offer of testing for women in antenatal clinics who refuse testing at booking. Repeat testing at 34-36 weeks' gestation should also be considered for women who initially test negative but have risk factors[24] such as a partner with HIV, because the high viral load associated with primary infection correlates with a high risk of HIV transmission from mother to child.

A point of care test should be recommended to women presenting to services for the first time in labour, as even at that stage preventive treatment preventive treatment can be given to reduce the risk of mother-to-child transmission.

see page 64 for clinicians' barriers to HIV testing

How to offer an HIV test

Clinicians may find it difficult to raise the issue of HIV testing with a patient. Here are some suggested approaches to broaching the subject.

When an HIV test is indicated by clinical symptoms, or by the diagnosis of an illness which could be attributable to a weakened immune system, the most straightforward way to approach the subject of a test is simply to state that an HIV test is recommended when these symptoms or conditions are present.

Examples of ways to phrase this are: 'These symptoms are usually caused by viral infections. While there are many viruses we can't test for, it's important to rule out the ones we can test for. HIV is one of these,' or 'I have no idea if you are at risk of HIV infection and I'm not making any assumptions but your symptoms suggest a weakened immune system and I'd like to make sure that I haven't missed anything'.

Similarly, in an antenatal clinic the midwife could say: 'We always recommend HIV testing for pregnant women because for mothers with HIV we can provide treatment to prevent them passing HIV to their babies'. In a dialysis unit the clinician could state: 'We routinely screen everyone in this clinic for HIV and for hepatitis B and C before starting treatment'. In a dermatology outpatient clinic a clinician might say: 'We always screen for HIV in patients who have shingles, because very occasionally this can be associated with HIV and we want to make sure that we don't miss anything'.

Offering and recommending testing to patients from groups at higher risk of HIV infection and who are attending healthcare services for reasons which are ostensibly or, in fact, unrelated to HIV can be more difficult as the patient may not be expecting to hear this. Consider the case of a man from Malawi presenting at the emergency department with a broken ankle

Omission of sexual history taking should not prevent HIV testing

- If a clinician believes that HIV may be part of a differential diagnosis, HIV testing should be recommended whether or not a sexual history is taken.

HIV testing may be the last thing he wants to think about or considers relevant to his needs at the time.

Nonetheless, where there are good epidemiological reasons for recommending testing to patients from higher-risk groups, the subject can be raised by stating that clearly and without judgement: 'I realise this might not be the first thing on your mind, but have you considered an HIV test? I ask because we know that there is a high rate of HIV among gay men/ people from [country of high prevalence] and we want to make sure that anybody who needs it gets the care they need as early as possible.'

It can also be useful to say that there are new HIV testing guidelines which recommend this as part of good medical practice as a way of reassuring the patient that you are not making judgements.

SECTION 3

How to diagnose HIV in non-HIV specialist secondary care settings

IN THIS SECTION

How to diagnose HIV in non-HIV specialist secondary care settings

The *UK National Guidelines for HIV Testing 2008* contain a table of clinical indicator diseases for adult HIV infection, and a separate table for paediatric HIV infection. The table is divided by medical specialty area and the nine specialties listed in the table are those in which undiagnosed HIV infection is most likely to be encountered. It lists AIDS-defining conditions as well as other conditions in which HIV should enter the differential diagnosis and therefore prompt the offer of an HIV test. The table is reproduced at the end of this booklet.

This section of the booklet provides a basic overview of the common presentations suggestive of HIV infection that the generalist or non-HIV specialist clinician in secondary care might encounter. It is divided by specialty, following those in the guidelines, and provides further information about how these conditions present in the HIV-infected patient. A section for acute and emergency medicine gives information on presentations which are suggestive of HIV infection and advice on testing, and a separate section on paediatrics provides some background information on HIV in children.

Inevitably, information on some conditions provided in particular specialty-specific sections will also be useful to other specialists or to generalists. Some cross-referencing is offered but the most comprehensive information will be obtained by looking through the whole of Section 3.

3.1 Acute and emergency medicine

Offering HIV testing in the emergency department (ED) may be difficult because of the lack of private space for confidential discussion, the busy setting and difficulty in following up patients. However, individuals with undiagnosed HIV may attend emergency services for completely unrelated medical or social reasons, or may have signs or symptoms suggestive of HIV infection. Therefore, when warranted as part of the differential diagnosis, HIV testing should be considered.

If the ED is able to deal with the patient's presenting condition and

Acute HIV-related conditions that may present in the emergency department

- Community acquired bacterial pneumonia. People with HIV, regardless of their level of immunosuppression, are more at risk of bacterial pneumonia. They have similar signs and symptoms to the non-HIV-infected population, eg fever, cough, dyspnoea, increased respiratory rate and sputum production.
- TB presents with malaise, weight loss, night sweats, fever, cough, sputum production (may be blood-stained), and lymphadenopathy.
- Pneumocystis pneumonia (PCP) presents with exertional dyspnoea, fever, dry cough, normal auscultation. X-ray typically shows perihilar shadowing (ground glass haze), but may be normal.
- Cryptococcal meningitis. This presents with headache, with or without classical signs of meningism. Occasionally rapid progression occurs, and the patient may present in coma.
- Cerebral toxoplasmosis. This may present with headache, fever, lethargy and confusion, progressing to fits and coma.

discharge them, and HIV is suspected, referral for HIV testing in a more appropriate setting such as a GUM clinic, infectious disease unit or primary care should be considered.

Every ED should know who is on call for HIV-infected patients locally, and those teams can offer advice about the need for urgent testing. Some EDs may be able to offer rapid testing, but if the ED is unable to perform the test and the hospital has a sexual health clinic or infectious disease unit the health adviser or specialist nurse can visit them to arrange the test in the ED and then follow up the result.

If the patient requires admission and HIV is suspected, documenting the need for HIV testing for the acute team to consider is recommended. The on-call medical team can also access emergency testing if clinically indicated via their local virology department and these results should be available within 24 hours.

Another important reason why EDs may have to test someone for HIV is if they present for post-exposure prophylaxis following sexual exposure (PEPSE). The BASHH guideline for the use of PEPSE stipulates that it should be commenced within 72 hours of exposure and, for optimal efficiency, within 24 hours. EDs are therefore expected to provide PEPSE when GUM/HIV services are closed. The guideline also states that it is mandatory to test individuals for whom PEPSE is provided, using a test with rapid result, prior to or shortly after commencing therapy[20].

see page 73 for PEP and exposure incidents

HIV-related presentations

Non-specific generalised flu-like symptoms can be associated with HIV either during primary HIV infection or with advanced symptomatic HIV.

Presentation is not HIV-related

Mr A, a 28-year-old man from Zimbabwe, presented to the ED on a busy Saturday evening with acute back pain. He had felt his back 'give' whilst lifting a heavy sofa. On examination he was diagnosed with mild musculo-skeletal pain and was prescribed ibuprofen. The doctor then noticed some small raised purple lesions on his face, which the patient said had been present for several months. On further questioning, the patient said that he had been feeling very run down over the past six months, and had lost about 10kg in weight. He had put this down to stress, as he was waiting for an asylum decision. He had also been worrying about his family in Zimbabwe, where his wife had recently been diagnosed with TB. The doctor then examined him more carefully. He had oral thrush and cervical lymphadenopathy.

Learning points

- HIV should be considered in people from areas of high HIV prevalence, regardless of their presentation.
- The presence of conditions that are possibly HIV-related can be used to initiate discussions about HIV testing.

see page 44 in section 3.11 for signs of primary HIV infection

They can also be due to a related opportunistic infection or a tumour. Consider offering an HIV test for people who present at the ED with symptoms such as:

- fever
- weight loss
- night sweats
- skin problems (especially shingles)
- oral candida
- lymphadenopathy.

3.2 Respiratory medicine

From the early stage of HIV infection, patients are vulnerable to pathogens of the respiratory tract.

HIV-related presentations

Pneumocystis pneumonia (PCP)

With CD4 counts below 200 cells/mm^3, pneumonia due to *Pneumocystis jirovecii* (previously known as *Pneumocystis carinii* and still commonly abbreviated to PCP) is common. It is a life-threatening infection and has a significant mortality rate. Symptoms are insidious in onset. PCP may be the first HIV-related clinical problem the patient develops and the earlier the infection is identified and treated the lower the risk of death.

Symptoms
- persistent dry cough
- increasing shortness of breath or decreased exercise tolerance: 'I first noticed it when I ran for a bus, but now I feel short of breath just sitting'
- difficulty in taking a full breath
- fever
- diarrhoea.

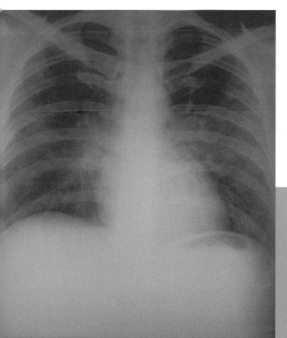

Assessment
The chest is often clear on auscultation although an increased respiratory rate is present. Fine crackles may be heard. Patients with PCP characteristically desaturate on exercise. PCP can be confused with asthma, commoner atypical chest infections and even anxiety.

Pneumocystis pneumonia in HIV

Mycobacterial infections

Mycobacterium tuberculosis. TB is an important and common disease in HIV-infected patients, especially those from countries which have a high TB prevalence. Atypical mycobacterial disease (*Mycobacterium avium-intracellulare*) is less common, and is associated with late stage HIV infection.

In early HIV infection, TB typically presents in a pattern characteristic of TB in the non-HIV-infected, with upper lung zone infiltrates, often with cavities. Cavities are a less common presentation of TB in the patient with a low CD4 cell count. These patients are more likely to present with either diffuse disease that may be miliary or with predominantly middle and lower lung zone infiltrates that can be mistaken for a bacterial pneumonia.

Symptoms

The patient may have a cough, fever, sweats, shortness of breath, weight loss and haemoptysis.

Extrapulmonary tuberculosis. The prevalence of extrapulmonary tuberculosis is increased in HIV-infected patients. Low CD4 counts are associated with an increased frequency of extrapulmonary tuberculosis and atypical chest radiographic findings, reflecting an inability of the impaired immune response to contain infection. Patients with extrapulmonary tuberculosis present with signs and symptoms specific to the involved site, such as lymphadenopathy, headache, meningism, pyuria, abscess formation, back pain and abdominal pain. These findings in HIV-infected patients can present a diagnostic challenge. Whenever possible, diagnostic specimens should be examined for acid-fast bacilli (AFB) and cultured for mycobacteria[25].

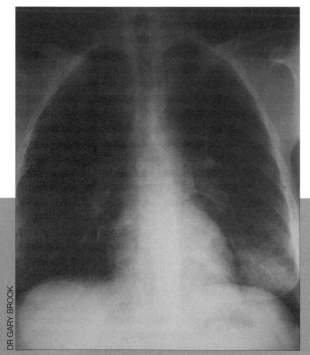

Tuberculosis in HIV – left lower lobe

DR GARY BROOK

Respiratory problems related to HIV

Infections

Bacterial
- Streptococcus pneumoniae
- Haemophilus influenzae
- Gram-negative bacilli (Pseudomonas aeruginosa, Klebsiella pneumoniae)
- Staphylococcus aureus

Mycobacterial
- Mycobacterium tuberculosis
- Mycobacterium avium-intracellulare (MAI), Mycobacterium avium complex (MAC)

Fungal
- Pneumocystis jirovecii
- Cryptococcus neoformans
- Aspergillus species
- Candida species

Viral
- Cytomegalovirus (CMV)
- Herpes simplex virus (HSV)

Parasitic
- Toxoplasma gondii
- Strongyloides stercoralis

Neoplasms
- Kaposi's sarcoma (KS)
- Non-Hodgkin's lymphoma (NHL)

Other respiratory illnesses

Upper respiratory
- Upper respiratory tract infection (URTI)
- Sinusitis
- Pharyngitis

Lower respiratory
- Lymphocytic interstitial pneumonitis (LIP)
- Non-specific interstitial pneumonitis (NIP)
- Acute bronchitis

Mycobacterium avium-intracellulare (MAI) – also called *Mycobacterium avium complex* (MAC). This may cause systemic symptoms including fever and diarrhoea. Chest symptoms may or may not be present. Abnormal liver function and anaemia may be found. *Mycobacterium avium-intracellulare* is very unlikely in a patient without several clinical pointers to HIV disease because it occurs at very low CD4 counts.

Assessment
Usual assessment for TB (chest X-ray, sputum analysis). The NICE guidelines for managing TB[26] recommend that all patients with TB are risk assessed for HIV.

'Ordinary' chest infections
The commonest organisms causing lung infections in the general population, eg *Streptococcus pneumoniae* and *Haemophilus influenzae,* are also a major cause of chest infections in immunocompromised patients. They present with symptoms similar to those seen in HIV-negative

SECTION 3

Chest infection

Mr B, aged 36, was referred to the local ED by his GP. He gave a 10-day history of increasing dyspnoea and non-productive cough, unresponsive to oral amoxicillin, on the background of several weeks of fever with sweats and weight loss of 5kg. On examination he was cyanosed, and there were fine crackles in both lung bases. A CXR showed bilateral diffuse infiltrates, O_2 saturation 90 per cent on room air PaO_2 (on air) = 7.9 kPa, WBC = 12.3 (90 per cent = neutrophils). The initial diagnosis was severe community-acquired pneumonia and the patient was admitted to hospital by the general medical team, given supplemental oxygen by face mask, and parenteral cefuroxime and clarithromycin.

On the 'post take' ward round the next morning he was re-assessed. He remained hypoxaemic and re-examination revealed oral hairy leukoplakia and marked oral candidiasis. Underlying immune suppression was suspected. Treatment was changed to IV high dose co-trimoxazole with adjuvant glucocorticoids. At bronchoscopy a few days later cysts of *Pneumocystis jirovecii* were identified in lavage fluid – confirming a diagnosis of Pneumocystis pneumonia (PCP).

After discussion with the medical team the patient agreed to an HIV test. He reported that he had had receptive unprotected anal intercourse with several male partners following the breakdown of a long-term relationship some six years previously. The HIV test was positive and a CD4 count was 120 cells/mm³. The patient was referred to the HIV specialist team and, following completion of treatment for PCP, began combination antiretroviral therapy. On the advice of the HIV team he gave permission for all results to be shared with his GP.

> Make sure that the discharge summary sent to the GP includes reason for admission, the HIV diagnosis, medication details and arrangements for follow-up.

Learning points

- Consider PCP in patients with recent onset dyspnoea or where atypical or severe respiratory infection is possible.
- People diagnosed with HIV-related problems should be referred urgently for specialist evaluation, preferably within 48 hours.
- Make sure that the discharge summary sent to the GP includes reason for admission, the HIV diagnosis, medication details and arrangements for follow-up.

patients but may be difficult to distinguish from other OIs on X-rays, in particular *H. influenzae* which can appear similar to PCP.

Aspergillosis

Exposure to *Aspergillus* is universal, but aspergillosis is rare without significant immunodeficiency and is only seen in patients with prolonged severe immunosuppression.

3.3 Neurology and psychiatry

HIV-related presentations

Neurological complications are common in those infected with HIV.

Some neurological manifestations result from a direct encephalitic effect of HIV and others from local neoplastic lesions and infectious lesions. Focal lesions are most commonly due to *Toxoplasma gondii*, cytomegalovirus, herpes simplex virus and lymphomas. Meningitis is most commonly caused by *Cryptococcus neoformans* and more rarely due to tuberculosis or bacterial infections.

Neuropathies

Peripheral neuropathies are common in HIV-infected patients and may be a result of:

- HIV
- opportunistic infection
- a complication of medication (mainly associated with didanosine and stavudine, and less commonly with lamivudine)
- nutritional deficiency (eg B12 or folate deficiency).

HIV-related conditions that may present in a neurology clinic

- Toxplasmosis presents with focal neurology evolving over a few days.
- Cryptococcal meningitis presents with headaches. Meningeal symptoms may be absent. Occasionally the patient may present in coma.
- Cytomegalovirus (CMV) encephalitis presents with confusion, lethargy, cranial nerve palsies and nystagmus; it occurs with advanced immunosuppression.
- HIV encephalopathy presents with cognitive and motor impairment.
- Progressive multifocal leucoencephalopathy (PML) presents with weakness, headaches, speech impairment, altered vision and weight loss. Caused by a human polyomavirus (JC virus).

- Primary cerebral lymphoma (also known as primary CNS lymphoma (PCNSL)) is a cause of cerebral mass lesions in patients with advanced HIV disease. The most common signs and symptoms are confusion, lethargy, and personality changes or focal deficits, eg hemiparesis, hemisensory loss, ataxia, and aphasia.

Other neurological conditions that can be associated with HIV

- Aseptic meningitis/encephalitis
- Cerebral abscess
- Space-occupying lesion of unknown cause
- Guillain-Barré Syndrome
- Transverse myelitis
- Peripheral neuropathy
- Dementia
- Leucoencephalopathy

Patients may present with:
- Guillain-Barré syndrome
- Transverse myelitis.

HIV encephalopathy

HIV encephalopathy, also known as HIV or AIDS-related dementia, is one of the most common and clinically important CNS complications of late HIV infection. While its pathogenesis remains unclear it is generally though to be caused by HIV itself, rather than another opportunistic infection.

Neurosyphilis

In the United Kingdom, there has been a recent resurgence of syphilis. Gay men have been disproportionately affected and around half of these men were HIV-positive. Therefore, there should be a high index of suspicion of HIV after any presentation of syphilis.

Symptomatic early neurosyphilis is a manifestation that usually occurs within the first 12 months of infection. Symptoms include meningitis, cranial and optic nerve function abnormalities, uveitis and stroke.

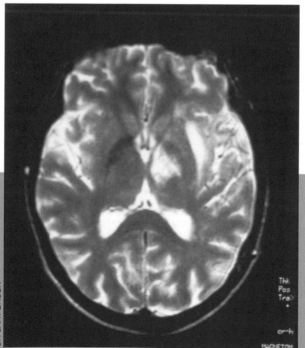

MRI scan of progressive multifocal leucoencephalopathy

DR GARY BROOK

3.4 Dermatology

HIV-related conditions that may present in a dermatology clinic

Fungal/yeast
- Candida (oral or oesophageal)
- Tinea infections (corporis, cruris, pedis, interdigitale etc)
- Pityriasis versicolor
- Seborrhoeic dermatitis (especially when severe or recalcitrant)
- Pityrosporum folliculitis

Viral
- Herpes zoster
- Herpes simplex
- Viral wart infections
- Molluscum contagiosum

Bacterial
- *Staphylococcus aureus*-impetigo, chronic folliculitis

Mycobacterial
- *M tuberculosis*

Infestations
- Scabies (especially Norwegian scabies)

Other
- Psoriasis
- Kaposi's sarcoma
- Acne

All of these skin conditions can occur without HIV, but consider HIV particularly if they are recalcitrant, recurrent or atypical.

HIV-related presentations

Skin conditions occur in more than 90 per cent of people with HIV during the course of their infection. Some people have an exacerbation of a pre-existing condition, such as psoriasis. This often occurs when the patient becomes increasingly immunocompromised. Others may have new skin problems, most of which are commonly found in the general population, although some, such as Kaposi's sarcoma, are strongly suggestive of associated HIV infection.

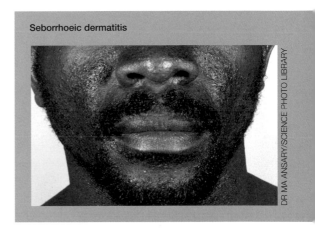

Seborrhoeic dermatitis

DR MA ANSARY/SCIENCE PHOTO LIBRARY

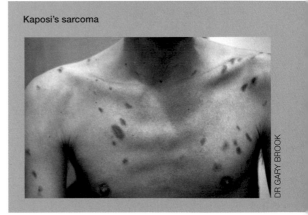

Kaposi's sarcoma

DR GARY BROOK

SECTION 3

Common skin problems

Mr G was a 19-year-old student. He had returned two weeks previously from his gap year in Malawi, where he had taught secondary school English. He had had mild psoriasis since age 10, which was well-controlled whilst he was in Africa. Immediately after returning his skin had flared up worse than ever before. He was single, a non-smoker, and drank 20 units of alcohol a week. He was referred by his GP to the dermatology clinic. The registrar treated him for psoriasis with topical corticosteroids and vitamin D analogues and arranged review in two weeks.

On review his rash was worse and he was pyrexial with enlarged cervical glands. Another doctor examined him and recognised that the rash was morbilliform and not typical of a psoriasis exacerbation. The doctor asked Mr G about his sexual history. He said that he had had a girlfriend in Malawi, and that they did not always use condoms. He had never had any sexually transmitted infections. The doctor took blood for appropriate tests which confirmed primary HIV infection. Mr G was distraught when he got the results and initially stated that he did not want anyone to be told about his result, including his GP. He was referred to the HIV specialist team and, after further discussion of the issues with the health adviser, he agreed that it was in his best interests to inform his GP.

> Mr G was distraught when he got the results and initially stated that he did not want anyone to be told about his result, including his GP.

Learning points

- HIV infection can often exacerbate common skin conditions.
- People diagnosed with HIV in any setting should be referred for specialist evaluation within a maximum of two weeks, preferably within 48 hours (national *Standards for HIV Clinical Care*).
- Although sometimes people with newly-diagnosed HIV are initially reluctant to share their HIV result with their GP, it is almost always in the patient's best interest to establish normal communication with the GP.

3.5 Gastroenterology and hepatology

HIV-related presentations

Diarrhoea

Acute or chronic diarrhoea can be a feature of HIV at any stage of the infection. Diarrhoea is most commonly due to an infection and much more rarely due to HIV enteropathy or malignancies such as Kaposi's sarcoma, lymphoma or bowel cancer. Symptoms of colitis or small-bowel watery diarrhoea are common, and often very distressing.

Oesophageal candidiasis

This is seen in patients with a low CD4 count, high viral load and neutropenia. It presents with dysphagia, odynophagia, retrosternal pain, nausea and vomiting. Oropharyngeal candidiasis is nearly always present.

Cholangitis

Patients with HIV can also present with cholangitis secondary to opportunistic infections such as CMV, cryptosporidiosis or microsporidial infection (usually in those who are severely immunocompromised).

Hepatitis

Co-infection of HIV with hepatitis B and/or C is not unusual and the infections share the same risk factors.

Causes of diarrhoea in people with HIV

Bacterial
- *Campylobacter* and *Salmonella* species are more likely to produce bacteraemia in people with HIV. Consider HIV testing in anyone with salmonella bacteraemia
- Enteroaggregative *Escherichia coli* (EAggEC) and other *E coli*
- *Clostridium difficile*

Protozoal
- *Cryptosporidium* species (AIDS-defining when persistent)
- *Giardia lamblia*
- *Isospora belli*
- *Entamoeba histolytica*
- *Microsporidium* species (only in severely immunocompromised)

Mycobacterial
- *Mycobacterium avium-intracellulare* (MAI) (only in severely immunocompromised)

Viral
- Adenovirus
- CMV (only in severely immunocompromised)

Non-infectious
- Kaposi's sarcoma
- Lymphoma
- Cytopathic effects of HIV – chronic diarrhoea of unknown cause, weight loss of unknown cause

---

SECTION 3

case study

Hepatitis C co-infection

A 35-year-old man, Mr C, was referred by his GP to the gastroenterology clinic. He had been complaining of tiredness and general malaise for several months and the only abnormality the GP had found was mildly elevated liver enzymes. He acknowledged having used intravenous drugs a few times as a teenager and was tested for hepatitis C and HIV infection. Hepatitis C antibody was detectable, his liver function tests were mildly abnormal and his subsequent liver biopsy revealed early fibrosis. He was referred for treatment of his hepatitis C with interferon and ribavirin.

His HIV test was also positive with a CD4 count of 550 cells/mm^3 and an HIV viral load of 2,000 copies/ml. He was referred to the specialist HIV unit to be assessed for ART.

He was also offered advice about reducing his alcohol intake and reducing the risk of transmitting HIV and hepatitis C to future partners. Patients who have hepatitis C and HIV are more likely to transmit hepatitis C sexually.

Learning points

- Improved survival of patients with HIV means that hepatitis C co-infection should be actively sought and treated to prevent progression to cirrhosis and hepatocellular carcinoma.
- Co-infected patients should be referred to the HIV specialist team as soon as possible for assessment for ART regardless of their CD4 count and viral load.

Co-infected patients have an increased risk of progressing to cirrhosis and developing hepatocellular carcinoma.

All patients with hepatitis B or C should be tested for HIV, as knowing about the dual diagnosis significantly alters the way both conditions are managed.

3.6 Oncology

HIV-related presentations

Some malignancies are clearly associated with HIV infection and their diagnosis classifies an HIV-infected patient as having developed AIDS. The three AIDS-defining cancers are:

- Kaposi's sarcoma
- non-Hodgkin's lymphoma
- cervical cancer.

However, there is an increasing number of other cancers which are more common in those with HIV than in the general population[27]. The cancers observed to occur more frequently in HIV-infected patients are:

- anal cancer and anal intraepithelial neoplasia (AIN)
- vaginal intraepithelial neoplasia (VIN)
- Hodgkin's lymphoma
- liver cancer
- lung cancer
- melanoma
- head and neck cancer
- oropharyngeal cancer
- colorectal cancer
- leukaemia
- renal cancer
- seminoma
- Castleman's disease.

As both Hodgkin's and non-Hodgkin's lymphomas are associated with HIV infection, the *UK National Guidelines for HIV Testing 2008* recommend that all individuals with lymphoma should be tested for HIV.

Primary CNS lymphoma is more common in HIV-infected patients than in the general population, although it is a feature of late-stage disease.

In children with HIV, leiomyosarcoma and leiomyoma are also seen more commonly.

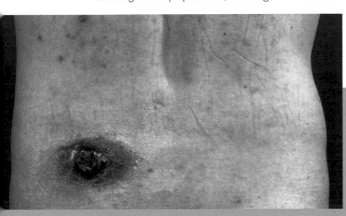

Cutaneous lymphoma

3.7 Obstetrics and gynaecology

Since 2000 there has been a universal antenatal screening policy for HIV. All pregnant women in the UK are routinely recommended and offered an HIV test during pregnancy[28].

Uptake of antenatal HIV testing is now over 90 per cent and more than 80 per cent of HIV infections in pregnant women are diagnosed prior to delivery.

The *UK National Guidelines for HIV Testing 2008* recommend universal HIV testing for all women attending termination of pregnancy services. This is based on evidence from unlinked anonymous seroprevalence surveys conducted in inner London termination clinics that there is a consistently higher prevalence of HIV infection in women terminating their pregnancies compared with those giving birth.

HIV-related presentations

Women with HIV, especially those with a low CD4 count, are more at risk from human papilloma virus (HPV)-related disease, including cervical intraepithelial neoplasia (CIN), cervical cancer, vaginal intraepithelial neoplasia (VIN) and genital warts. HIV should be considered in women with cervical cancer.

Incidental findings

HIV testing should also be considered in women with vaginal candidiasis, genital herpes and pelvic inflammatory disease (PID), particularly if the presentations are chronic or florid or if they have other HIV risk factors. Smear abnormalities suggestive of HPV infection should also prompt consideration of an HIV test.

The *UK National Guidelines for HIV Testing 2008* recommend that any diagnosis of a sexually transmitted infection should prompt the offer of an HIV test.

Some fertility clinics are now offering HIV testing as routine to patients.

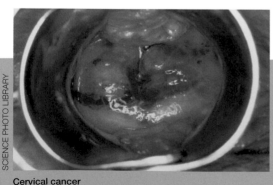

SCIENCE PHOTO LIBRARY

Cervical cancer

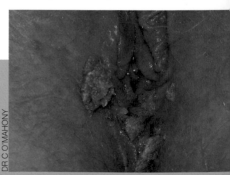

DR C O'MAHONY

Florid genital warts

3.8 Haematology

HIV-related presentations

Significant haematological abnormalities are common in those with HIV. Impaired haematopoiesis, immune-mediated cytopaenias (anaemia, thrombocytopenia, neutropenia and lymphopaenia) and altered coagulation mechanisms have all been described. These abnormalities may occur as a result of HIV infection itself, as sequelae of HIV-related infections or malignancies or as a consequence of drugs used to treat HIV infection and associated conditions. Changes on a routine blood count may therefore suggest HIV infection and it should be routinely considered in individuals with unexplained thrombocytopenia or neutropenia.

Anaemia is a common finding in patients with HIV, particularly in individuals with more advanced disease. A common infectious cause is *Mycobacterium avium-intracellulare* (MAI) and other causes are rarer, eg B19 parvovirus. Gastrointestinal (GI) bleeding can also be the cause of anaemia. In addition to the usual causes of gastrointestinal blood loss, HIV-related infections such as cytomegalovirus colitis and malignancies such as Kaposi's sarcoma and non-Hodgkin's lymphoma may produce clinically significant GI bleeding in people with HIV.

Thrombocytopenia is frequently associated with HIV infection. Possible aetiologies include immune-mediated destruction, thrombotic thrombocytopaenic purpura, impaired haematopoiesis, and toxic effects of medications. Often, however, thrombocytopenia is an isolated haematologic abnormality associated with normal or increased megakaryocytes in the bone marrow and elevated levels of platelet-associated immunoglobulin. These patients have the clinical syndrome commonly referred to as immune thrombocytopaenic purpura (ITP).

Neutropenia and **lymphopaenia** are common in those with HIV infection. Low lymphocyte counts often reflect a low CD4 count and this should prompt HIV testing. There is a high incidence of neutropenia and lymphopaenia in those with more profound immunodeficiency.

3.9 Ophthalmology

HIV-related conditions that may present in an ophthalmology clinic

Protozoal
- *Toxoplasma gondii*

Viral
- Herpes zoster ophthalmicus
- Herpes simplex keratitis
- CMV retinitis
- Herpes simplex virus
- Herpes zoster virus retinitis

Fungal
- Microsporidial keratoconjunctivitis

Other
- Kaposi's sarcoma
- Lymphoma

HIV
- Can cause retinal haemorrhages and cotton wool spots, and rarely optic neuropathy
- Retinal arterial occlusion

HIV-related presentations

Unexplained or atypical retinopathies or uveitis may indicate underlying HIV infection. HIV itself commonly causes retinal haemorrhage and cotton wool spots and rarely optic neuropathy. Kaposi's sarcoma may spread to involve the conjunctivae, eyelids and orbit in patients who are severely immunocompromised.

Vision can also be compromised by infections with cytomegalovirus (CMV), herpes simplex virus, syphilis, herpes zoster virus and *Toxoplasma gondii*.

CMV retinitis can cause blindness untreated. It is usually seen in severely immunocompromised patients with a CD4 count of less than 100 cells/mm^3. CMV retinitis may be the first presentation for people with HIV.

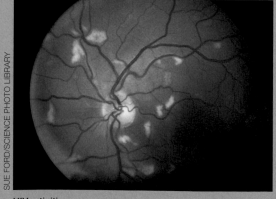

HIV retinitis

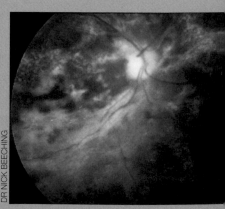

CMV retinitis

3.10 Ear, nose and throat

HIV-related presentations

Signs of HIV infection are commonly found in the mouth:

- oral candidiasis
- aphthous ulceration
- recurrent severe herpes simplex infection
- oral hairy leukoplakia is pathognomonic of immunosuppression
- gingivitis, especially if necrotising or ulcerative
- Kaposi's sarcoma
- dental abscess
- chronic parotitis. In some studies 40 per cent of children with HIV have parotid enlargement, with a median time from birth to development of 4.6 years. Parotitis in children is associated with a slower rate of disease progression.

HIV should also be considered in patients with persistent cervical lymphadenopathy, which may be due to HIV itself or secondary to infections (especially TB) and tumours (especially lymphoma).

Infection or inflammation of the sinuses is a common problem among people with HIV and its severity increases in people with lower CD4 cell counts.

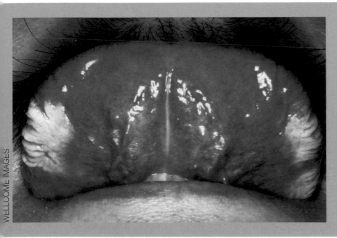

Oral hairy leukoplakia

WELLCOME IMAGES

3.11 Other presentations where HIV testing should be routinely offered

The *UK National Guidelines for HIV Testing 2008* list several other conditions which should prompt consideration of HIV infection if they are present. Oral candidiasis and oral hairy leukoplakia are covered in Section 3.10 (Ear, nose and throat).

Primary HIV infection

Although the opportunity to diagnose primary HIV infection is limited by the short duration of the symptoms and their non-specific nature, making the diagnosis correctly is valuable because:

- the next opportunity for diagnosis may be at a late stage of disease progression, and so the prognosis for the patient is likely to be worse
- early detection may protect other people from becoming infected as at the time of seroconversion the patient may be very infectious.

If you suspect primary HIV infection

- A useful rule of thumb is that if you are considering glandular fever (mononucleosis) then you should also consider primary HIV infection.
- Take a history and conduct an examination to look for evidence of primary HIV infection.
- Symptoms can be non-specific, but include fever, sore throat, malaise or lethargy, arthralgia and myalgia, headache and cervical lymphadenopathy.
- Symptoms and signs that are more specific to primary HIV infection include rash affecting the trunk, and orogenital or perianal ulceration. Diarrhoeal illness or aseptic meningitis may occur.
- The CD4 count may drop acutely at this stage of HIV infection, and so acute conditions associated with immunosuppression may occur.
- If you remain concerned, raise the subject with the patient, eg 'Illnesses like this are usually caused by viruses – the glandular fever or flu virus. Some quite rare viruses can also be a cause, such as HIV and we routinely check for HIV in cases like this'.

Pyrexia of unknown origin

Pyrexia of unknown origin (PUO) covers a broad range of possible diagnoses.

PUO in inpatients who have not been diagnosed with HIV should therefore prompt consideration of HIV infection and inclusion of HIV testing in their investigations (see above). PUO in the context of a tropical infectious disease should also prompt consideration of HIV in patients who have been abroad recently and who present with symptoms.

In patients with advanced HIV infection prolonged febrile episodes are frequent. The causes are mainly the result of opportunistic infections or malignancies and rarely are due to HIV itself.

Any sexually transmitted infection

The British Association for Sexual Health and HIV recommends that all patients presenting to GUM settings with symptoms of a

HIV FOR NON-HIV SPECIALIST

case study

Primary HIV infection

Miss J was a 30-year-old university lecturer who presented at the ED with a five-day history of fever, headache, sore throat and a sore mouth. She said she was worried that she might have malaria, as she had returned from a safari holiday in Namibia about 10 days previously, although she had taken antimalarials as prescribed whilst away. On examination, Miss J was pyrexial with mouth ulcers. The malaria slide and malarial antigen tests were negative, her ESR was raised and she had slight neutropenia. Miss J agreed to have an HIV test. The p24 antigen was positive and the HIV antibody test negative, confirming primary HIV infection. She then stated that she had had unprotected sex with the tour guide whilst on her safari.

Learning point
- Consider primary HIV infection in people with fever returning from overseas travel to areas of high HIV prevalence.

sexually transmitted infection (STI), or for a routine STI screen, should be tested for HIV.

The behavioural risk factors for most STIs are the same as those for HIV (unprotected vaginal or anal intercourse) and this should prompt an HIV test even in those patients who do not belong to one of the main at-risk populations.

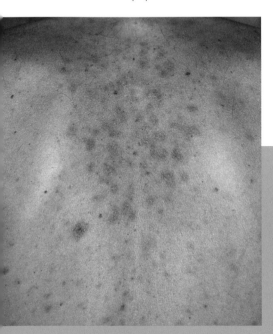

Primary HIV Infection rash

3.12 Paediatrics

written by Dr Hermione Lyall, Family HIV Centre, St Mary's Hospital, London

There are currently around 1,200 HIV-infected children living in the UK and Ireland. All infants born to mothers with HIV and all children diagnosed with HIV are reported to the national cohort (for more details see www.nshpc.ucl.ac.uk and www.chipscohort.ac.uk). Children may be diagnosed with HIV because they present with symptoms or because they are tested after their parents or siblings are found to be HIV-infected.

Infants are at particular risk of severe HIV disease and up to 20 per cent will develop an AIDS diagnosis or die within the first year of life if they do not receive appropriate treatment. Infants most often present with PCP, CMV disease, HIV encephalopathy, and/or failure to thrive.

After the first year of life older children may present with recurrent infections (eg of the ear, chest or skin) or more severe manifestations of common childhood infections (eg severe chicken pox). A common presentation of HIV in children is with chronic painless swelling of the parotid glands (the glands in front of the ears which enlarge with mumps), as well as chronic enlargement of the cervical glands and recurrent upper respiratory infections. This is often accompanied by lymphoid interstitial pneumonitis (LIP) where there is infiltration of the lungs with nodules of inflammatory lymphocytes. This is usually asymptomatic, but has a characteristic

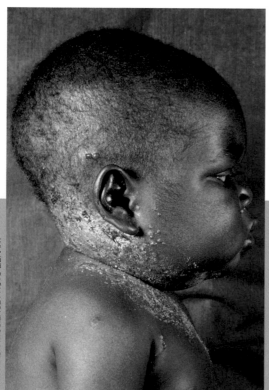

DR MA ANSARY/SCIENCE PHOTO LIBRARY

Paediatric shingles

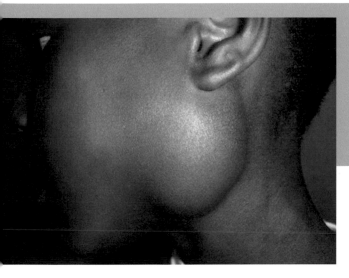

Paediatric parotid swelling

appearance on chest X-ray which can be difficult to distinguish from miliary tuberculosis. Children of any age with more advanced immunodeficiency may present with AIDS diagnoses similar to those seen in adults.

With access to treatment and adequate adherence support infants and children respond very well to ART with the prospect of long-term survival into adult life. Treatment of HIV in children in the UK is managed within the Children's HIV National Network (CHINN) and led by paediatric infectious disease specialists working alongside local teams according to where the child lives. Children with HIV should be treated according to the Paediatric European Network for the Treatment of AIDS (PENTA) guidelines[29] which are endorsed by the Children's HIV Association of the UK and Ireland (CHIVA).

Consider HIV in children if a parent is diagnosed

If an adult is diagnosed with HIV then they must always be asked if they have children.

Children and young people may be infected with HIV and never have presented with symptoms even up to 20 years of age. Therefore, whatever a child or young person's age, if a family member has been diagnosed with HIV then they should always be recommended a test.

case study

Late diagnosis in a child

Mrs O had lived in the UK for 10 years, and was originally from Uganda. She brought her 14-year-old niece, B, to the GP's surgery as she was worried about some painful spots on her leg. The GP diagnosed shingles affecting L2-4 dermatomes and the lesions resolved after treatment with acyclovir.

On review, Mrs O informed the GP that B had arrived in the UK six months previously to live with her as her own mother had recently died of tuberculosis. Her father had died of cancer four years previously, and her baby brother had died of pneumonia seven years ago at three months of age.

The GP recommended that with B's recent shingles and her family history, she should have an HIV test. She performed the test herself and when the result came back it was positive.

Learning points

- Some children with HIV only present with symptoms in the second decade of life.
- Always take a family history; this may identify risk factors for HIV in a child with or without significant symptoms.

case study

HIV infection during pregnancy

Ms S had a negative HIV test in pregnancy when she was booked at 12 weeks. By the time her baby, A, was 14 weeks old he had been treated twice by the GP for oral thrush which had persisted. Two days ago A was admitted to the Paediatric Intensive Care Unit (PICU) with severe pneumonia, now very ill and on a ventilator. The PICU doctor informed Ms S that A had a very severe kind of pneumonia called PCP, which usually only occurs in infants with immune deficiency. The doctor advised that his immune system needed to be tested and that this would involve an HIV test.

Ms S explained that she had had a negative HIV test in pregnancy so she did not think that A could have HIV. The doctor explained that if a mother becomes infected with HIV during pregnancy or whilst breastfeeding then she has a high chance of passing it to her baby, as during primary HIV infection there is a very high level of the virus in her blood which could infect the baby during birth, and in the breast milk which may pass to the baby during feeding.

Ms S then told the doctor that A's father was from Zimbabwe and that he had returned from a three-month visit there when she was seven months pregnant. She agreed to the HIV test and the result was positive.

> Even though a mother has had a negative HIV test at booking this does not mean her infant cannot have HIV

Learning points

- Even though a mother has had a negative HIV test at booking this does not mean her infant cannot have HIV.
- Pregnant and lactating women should be advised to have protected sex to prevent transmission of sexually transmitted infections which may cause disease in mother and foetus/baby (eg HIV, syphilis, gonorrhoea, chlamydia).

SECTION 4

Pre-test discussion

Pre-test discussion

The term 'pre-test discussion' is considered to be more appropriate than 'pre-test counselling'[7,8,9,10] which was previously used and implied the need for in-depth counselling by a specially-trained healthcare worker. For the clinician, the main reason for a pre-test discussion is to ensure the patient's informed consent to be tested for HIV. However, for the patient it is an opportunity to consider the possible outcomes and their consequences in the broader context of their own lives. The time a discussion may take is variable. With a well-informed, reasonably low-risk person the discussion may take just a minute or two, but with a person from a marginalised group with a high risk of HIV infection there are many factors which can impact upon their decision to take an HIV test. These are discussed more fully in section 6.

see page 22 for how to offer an HIV test

It is helpful to give the patient printed information on HIV testing in your service which you can go through with them. This will help you ensure you have covered all the necessary areas before proceeding with the test. The following is a breakdown of the essential areas that need to be covered in a pre-test discussion.

Discuss the benefits of performing an HIV test
As when proposing any clinical investigation it is important to inform the patient of the rationale for testing in a manner which is appropriate to their situation.

see page 60 for patients' barriers to HIV testing

There are various reasons why a patient may be apprehensive about taking an HIV test so you should be clear with them about the medical advantage of knowing their HIV status. The advantage of early detection and referral for treatment, referral for support services and prevention of transmission to sexual partners should be emphasised.

Some patients, particularly those who are asymptomatic, may believe they are better off not knowing. Others may fear stigma, discrimination, loss of employment, or the detrimental impact of a positive test result on immigration procedures, so reassurance about confidentiality is important.

Such concerns should be listened to, addressed and balanced against the significant advantages of knowing one's status if positive.

Some patients may find the use of the term 'positive' to be confusing and it has been known for patients to equate 'positive' with 'good news', and to assume therefore that they do not have HIV. This should be clarified, particularly for those for whom English is not their first language.

Make arrangements for giving the test result
Ideally the result is best given in person by the individual who performed the test, and in an environment where the discussion cannot be overheard. Give the patient the details of the appointment and who they

will be seeing to get the result. Record contact details, check the patient's preferred method of contact, and check for any possible problems with leaving messages or talking. This is particularly important if the patient fails to attend for a result that turned out to be positive.

Once informed consent is established, record in the notes that pre-test discussion has taken place and consent obtained. Record in the notes who is going to give the results and date of the appointment. Explain that a positive test result will need to be recorded in a patient's medical records so that their healthcare remains safe and appropriate. Also record if the patient has agreed for the results to be sent to any other healthcare professional involved in their care, eg their GP.

Written consent
Written consent is not required for an HIV test. The General Medical Council's guidance on consent, *Consent: patients and doctors making decisions together* contains the following statement which appears to imply that written consent would be needed:

'49. You should also get written consent from a patient if:
...b. there may be significant consequences for the patient's employment, or social or personal life'.

The GMC advises in the introduction to the document that '...'you should' is also used where the duty or principle will not apply in all situations or circumstances[30]' in discussion with the authors of the *UK National Guidelines for HIV Testing 2008* has agreed that this provision is adequate to exempt HIV testing from written consent requirements.

Patients who decline a test
Sometimes a patient will refuse a test and the reasons for this should be explored as they may have incorrect information about HIV transmission or the consequences of testing, such as concerns about confidentiality or insurance.

For patients who are at high risk of HIV infection but decline testing in your setting, it may be better to recommend referral to a specialist service (GUM clinic, infectious disease clinic or voluntary sector organisation) where they can discuss their concerns more fully and where additional support is available.

Where patients do not have English as a first language, it is advisable not to use family members or friends of the patient as interpreters when discussing HIV testing as this may breach confidentiality, so consider rescheduling an appointment with an interpreter from a recognised service.

It is important to bear in mind that, as with any investigation, patients have a right to refuse and are not obliged to give a reason. They should not be pressured or coerced into testing against their own judgement. If this happens, it is important to document this in the notes, along with any reasons the patient gives for declining the test.

SECTION 5

Post-test discussion

IN THIS SECTION

Post-test discussion

Giving a patient the result of an HIV test should be no more or less difficult than giving any other test result, especially when the result is negative. Giving a positive result will require your skills in breaking bad news to patients, and most clinicians will have to give test results which are life-altering and which can upset the patient at some point in their careers.

Whatever the result of the HIV test, clear procedures should be in place for giving results, as is the case with other tests. It is considered good practice to arrange with the patient how the result will be given when the test is taken and this is particularly important for outpatient and emergency care settings.

Some GUM clinics give negative HIV test results by phone or by text message to reduce the number of follow-up appointments a busy service has to make and if this is acceptable to the patient, your clinic or service may wish to consider this.

However, for certain groups of patients it is strongly recommended that any HIV test results are given in person. These are:
- ward-based patients
- those more likely to have an HIV-positive result
- those with mental health issues
- those for whom English is a second language
- young people under 16 years
- those who may be anxious or highly vulnerable.

Depending on how well you know the patient, the pre-test discussion may be the last opportunity to assess how they might react to the result, so it is important that you record in the notes of that discussion any signals the patient gave about their state of mind or level of vulnerability. This may include the need for early referral to support services within the hospital or to voluntary and community-based organisations.

Post-test discussion for individuals who test HIV-negative

If you have initiated an HIV test on clinical grounds, eg in order to exclude HIV from the differential diagnosis, giving a negative result should be straightforward and it is likely that you will need only to refer to your original grounds for testing to give it.

The *UK National Guidelines for HIV Testing 2008* refer to providing advice about minimising risk or behaviour change. This recommendation is appropriate to HIV testing in primary care settings. In a small number of situations, however, the secondary care generalist may have to offer an HIV test on account of a patient's behavioural risk factors in addition to being part of the clinical investigation. These factors may then have to be addressed when giving the test result. If you feel confident to provide such health promotion and advice, then it is good practice to do this yourself as part of the post-test discussion. This could include post-exposure prophylaxis (PEP) for those individuals at high risk of repeat exposure to HIV infection and referral to HIV prevention services including drug treatment/harm reduction programmes where appropriate. If you don't feel able to do this effectively, then refer the patient to GUM or HIV services or voluntary sector agencies.

The patient should understand the significance of the window period and be made aware that a repeat test may be needed if exposure has occurred within that time. Although the standard blood test for HIV can detect it as early as 28 days after exposure, it is currently recommended that the test is repeated if exposure has occurred within the last three months. Ensure that the patient understands that they may need a repeat test before HIV infection can be ruled out and that they should continue with safer sex practices to prevent onward transmission as, if they are infected, this is one of the most infectious stages of the disease. Once again, referral to the HIV specialist unit may be the most appropriate course of action.

Some HIV test results may be inconclusive, and are usually reported as 'reactive' or 'equivocal'. This could occur in a patient who has primary HIV infection presenting to emergency services. There are good reasons for detecting people with HIV as early as possible in the infection so such patients should be promptly referred to specialist HIV care for assessment and the management of re-testing.

Post-test discussion for individuals who test HIV-positive

Although no patient welcomes a life-altering diagnosis, the situation for people with HIV in the UK is much more optimistic than it was 20 or even 10 years ago. If patients are provided with clear information about the availability and effectiveness of antiretroviral therapy, and made aware of the possibility that they can continue working, have sexual relationships, conceive safely and have children with minimal risk of passing on HIV, many of their immediate fears will be alleviated. There are many agencies that support people and families affected with HIV. A list of national organisations, with websites and telephone contacts, is given at the end of this booklet.

see page 80 for details of national support services

If the result is positive, here are some things to consider before the patient attends.

Preparing to give a positive result

You will have time to seek advice if necessary because the lab is likely to phone the result through and ask for a repeat sample. If this is the first positive HIV test result you have had to give it may be possible to arrange for someone from the HIV specialist unit such as a clinical nurse specialist or health adviser to attend the consultation to assist you. Remember:

- you already have skills in discussing difficult issues with patients
- the patient agreed to do their test on your recommendation and will be expecting you to give them the result.

Referral arrangements

The national *Standards for HIV Clinical Care* (2007) recommend that any patient receiving a positive HIV test result in any setting should to be referred to a specialist HIV clinic within two weeks for assessment and management, and preferably within 48 hours. If you are giving a positive HIV test result in any secondary care setting you should ensure you have details of the nearest HIV specialist service so that an appointment can be made when the patient attends for their result.

When the patient attends

Give the result soon after the patient is in the room and is seated. Delaying disclosure can heighten anxiety. Some patients are expecting a positive result and may be quite calm. Some may have already come to terms with being positive, but a calm exterior can mask a sense of shock.

Tell the patient that their HIV care will be managed by the specialist team who will undertake a full assessment and be able to answer questions about prognosis, treatment options and reducing the risks of onward transmission so you will not need to be familiar with the complexities of these matters. Remember to re-emphasise that the patient is better off knowing that they have HIV than not knowing.

The *UK National Guidelines for HIV Testing 2008* also refer to providing detailed post-test discussion and partner notification. Once again, this is more likely to be relevant to HIV testing in primary care settings, but it is certainly the case that some people diagnosed in secondary care will need in-depth and ongoing counselling to help them cope following an HIV diagnosis. Referral to specialist counselling services or HIV support groups is appropriate and details of these will usually be available from GUM/HIV services.

When the consultation is coming to an end:

- give the patient the details of any referral arrangements/appointments that you have set up
- remind the patient that their future HIV care should be with the HIV specialist, whether or not you need to see them again.

It is possible that patients with HIV will be anxious about how their HIV status is to be kept in their records. It is best to raise the subject so that this issue can be addressed and the benefits outlined, as well as making clear the potential risks should the diagnosis not be clearly recorded.

The importance of informing and involving the GP

Tell the patient that it is standard practice for specialists to inform a patient's GP of the results of any test or procedure performed in hospital, and that the HIV specialist team will 'let the GP know about all your test results so that he/she can help in your future care'. Some patients may initially be reluctant to have their GP made aware of their positive HIV status, so you should highlight the advantages of sharing results with the GP. If a patient is not registered with a GP they should be encouraged to register and be given information on how to do this.

Benefits of involving the GP

It is important to emphasise the benefits of involving the GP because the GP:

- is increasingly expected to provide general medical care to those diagnosed with HIV
- is usually the first contact for out-of-hours and emergency care
- will need to be aware of any ART prescribed so that adverse drug interactions can be avoided when other drugs are prescribed
- is in close contact with local social, counselling and support services and can therefore refer for appropriate support if required
- can diagnose, treat or refer HIV-related problems which could be overlooked if he/she is unaware of the diagnosis
- can support the whole family, but will not tell other members of the family unless the patient requests it and will not do this without discussion.

It was previously the case that people with HIV used to have all their medical care managed in the HIV specialist setting, but due to changes in funding arrangements HIV specialist services are expected to provide only HIV and HIV-related treatment and care.

Non-attendance for HIV test results

Sometimes patients will not return to collect their HIV test result. This can occur whether the test result is positive or negative. There may be simple logistical reasons for this or it may be because they are worried about the impact of a positive result. There is usually a significant benefit for the patient in knowing the test result, both for those testing positive and those testing negative. The benefits to the patient of receiving a positive test result are clear, but there are also important benefits for those who test negative, eg relief of anxiety and increased motivation to use HIV preventive measures when in sexually high-risk or serodiscordant sexual relationships (where one partner is HIV-positive, the other HIV-negative).

It is good practice to have procedures in place to maximise follow-up for people who do not return for the results of any investigation carried out in a secondary care setting. HIV test results are no different in that patient contact details should be recorded and options for contact discussed. However, due to the sensitive nature of an HIV diagnosis and its attendant social implications, it is important to record during the pre-test discussion whether the patient has agreed that the result may be shared with their GP so that appropriate follow-up can occur.

Providing written confirmation of results

Patients may require a written confirmation of a negative HIV test result, eg for the purposes of employment, or for travel to a country with strict controls on admitting people with HIV. Also, patients who are diagnosed HIV-positive may request written confirmation of their HIV status – a 'letter of diagnosis' is usually required when applying for certain benefits, for example.

If there are sound lines of communication between primary and secondary care then such confirmations are better provided by the patient's GP, but if you are asked to do this it is good practice to have a procedure in place for such an eventuality. This involves:

- asking to see a form of photographic identification such as a passport or driving licence both at the time the test is taken and when the result is given
- documenting the patient's request and the form of identification both in the notes and in the letter provided
- providing a letter signed by the doctor – a copy of the patient's laboratory test result is not appropriate
- addressing the letter to a specific individual in the organisation requesting confirmation, not in general terms such as 'To whom it may concern'.

SECTION 6

Barriers to HIV testing

IN THIS SECTION

Barriers to HIV testing

The reasons why people may not agree to test for HIV when they might for other equally serious medical conditions are many and complex. This section is intended to give the non-specialist clinician an insight into these reasons and to provide some background on what might inform a patient's decision to test, or not to test, for HIV. In so doing, it looks at common barriers for patients to HIV testing.

Patient concerns about HIV testing
Confidentiality

see page 57 for benefits of involving the GP

Although the 'exceptionalism' associated with HIV, and HIV testing in particular, is now being challenged many people still worry about confidentiality and fear the consequences of others finding out if they test positive. As HIV remains a highly stigmatising diagnosis in the UK these fears are often not unfounded.

Concerns about the confidentiality of HIV test results can be a barrier to seeking HIV testing or agreeing to be tested. These concerns may also inhibit people from talking openly about personal issues, so it is important for clinicians who offer HIV testing to explore worries about confidentiality and reassure patients about local measures to protect confidentiality. If clinicians take a non-judgemental and empathic approach to different lifestyles this can help in allaying patients' fears. Ensuring that services understand and respect patient concerns about confidentiality and fears of discrimination will support and encourage:

- open discussion of, and testing for, HIV with those who may be at risk
- open discussion about safer sexual and injecting practices
- improved quality of care for people with HIV infection.

For updated guidance on confidentiality from the GMC[31] see its website.

case study

Fears about confidentiality

Mr and Mrs U are a middle aged couple who live in suburban London. They both have HIV and are on treatment. They have two teenage children; the older one is applying for medical school. They are terrified that their children, neighbours and friends might find out about their HIV. Mrs U attends an HIV clinic in central London where she has given a false name and keeps her ART in her handbag for fear of her children finding it and asking questions. She disposes of the packaging away from her home. *'I know if my neighbours found out they would not let their kids stay over at our place, and I am sure I would lose my job. I know that there are supposed to be laws to protect you but you can imagine what would happen – people wouldn't want someone with HIV serving food to their children'.*

Learning point
- Some patients will go to enormous lengths to protect their confidentiality.

HIV testing and insurance

It is still widely believed by the general public that having an HIV test will adversely affect life insurance or mortgage applications and this has led to a reluctance to test for HIV. This is because people are afraid that a doctor or patient may have to declare an HIV test regardless of the result on an insurance application. However, as long ago as 1994 the Association of British Insurers (ABI) stated that a previous negative HIV test should not affect an application for insurance[32]. Recent joint guidelines from the ABI and BMA provide more detailed advice for doctors. Insurers should only ask applicants whether they have tested positive for HIV[33].

Therefore, doctors should be guided by clinical need above all other considerations and not allow insurance concerns to compromise patient care. If an HIV test is appropriate, it should be offered and the patient reassured that negative test results will have no bearing on future life insurance applications.

Patients who ask should be informed that positive HIV test results, just like positive test results for any other serious medical condition, would have to be declared on such applications[34], but this is not a complete bar to obtaining insurance or mortgages and there are companies that offer these services to people with HIV.

Immigration issues

Testing and counselling for HIV are free to everyone regardless of their residence status. However, any subsequent treatment for HIV is not.

There are also other exemptions from NHS charging regulations. The main ones are:

- anyone living lawfully in the UK for the previous 12 months
- anyone in legal employment in the UK for a UK-based employer
- anyone taking up permanent residence in the UK (but applicants for permanent residence will be charged until it is granted or until 12 months of lawful residence is reached)
- refugees and asylum seekers
- prisoners and immigration detainees
- full-time students (they usually must be on courses of six months or more)
- anyone whose home countries have a reciprocal health agreement with the UK.

Many people who are seeking asylum in the UK come from high prevalence countries in sub-Saharan Africa and may worry that a positive HIV test may be detrimental in their asylum case. Having HIV is not a factor that will prevent asylum being granted and asylum seekers can claim free HIV treatment from the NHS as long as their claim is current, including any appeal periods. Asylum seekers who have already accessed free treatment and whose claim is later denied are still entitled to that course of treatment free of charge and, due to a High Court decision, as of April 11 2008 may potentially be considered to be ordinarily resident in

case study

Asylum seeker and HIV treatment

Dr H, aged 37, from Zambia, married with three children and in the UK studying for his MRCP was referred for treatment of his hypertension. He presented with widespread seborrhoeic dermatitis and cervical lymphadenopathy. When asked if he had had any medical problems in the past, he denied anything apart from his poorly controlled hypertension.

When an HIV test was suggested, he became very anxious. He said he was very worried about the possibility of HIV, and confided that he would find it very difficult to talk to his wife about it. He also feared that if the Home Office or his employer knew he had HIV, it could have detrimental implications for his continuing to remain in the UK. His younger sister had recently died of TB/HIV, shortly after giving birth to her first child in Zambia.

The doctor involved the HIV specialist team and the health adviser reassured Dr H that he was better off getting his HIV treated and that he was eligible for free treatment. He agreed to take the test and it was positive.

Learning points

- HIV prevalence is greater than 15 per cent among adults from some southern African countries.
- Fear of discrimination in immigration and employment can lead to denial about HIV.
- Complex issues should be referred to the HIV specialist team for discussion.

the UK regardless of the fact that their application has failed, in which case all treatment they need for any condition will be free.

However, for those whose claim has already been rejected who were not already receiving free HIV treatment and who are not considered to meet the ordinary residence test, free HIV treatment is not available. In some cases lawyers will try to argue that a person with HIV requiring treatment should not be deported to their country of origin if ART is not available there – however such arguments are often not successful in obtaining asylum for such applicants. Some women fleeing conflict zones may have added HIV risk, having suffered sexual violence. Discussing HIV in these situations must be approached sensitively and advice can be sought and counselling available from organisations such as the Medical Foundation for the Care of Victims of Torture.

As immigration is a complex and specialist topic, anyone seeking advice on their entitlement to free NHS treatment should contact the appropriate advice services.

Criminal prosecution of HIV transmission

see page 80 for details of national support services

Between 2001 and 2008 there were 16 prosecutions in the UK for transmitting HIV during unprotected sex. In England and Wales those found guilty were convicted of 'recklessly inflicting grievous bodily harm', under Section 20 of the Offences Against the Person Act 1861, and in Scotland of 'reckless injury'. The majority of these prosecutions have resulted in prison sentences ranging from two to ten years. It should be borne in mind that such prosecutions are rare unless there are compelling circumstances and there is no offence of exposure to HIV. No prosecutions have been brought where transmission has not occurred.

In one case the defendant had never had an HIV test, but it was judged that he ought to have known or suspected that he had HIV. In several cases, analysis of virus samples from the complainant and defendant was used to 'prove' that the defendant infected the complainant[35]. However, in one case it was established that such analysis is incapable of proving conclusively that one party infected the other and the defendant was acquitted. Where, however, the strains are different, analysis can prove conclusively that one party did not infect the other[36].

HIV support organisations fear that any criminal prosecution of HIV transmission increases stigma and marginalisation for people with HIV, and prevents people who may be at risk from seeking testing and care[37].

These legal cases have raised concerns for clinicians and patients about their rights, responsibilities and legal obligations to disclose information to others, particularly as confidential medical records can be obtained by a court order for use as evidence in trials. These concerns are discussed in detail in a briefing paper[38] which outlines how decisions often have to be taken in situations of legal and ethical uncertainty.

Stigma

HIV and AIDS are predominantly found in marginalised groups in society such as gay men and immigrants, or associated with behaviours such as casual sex, drug addiction, prostitution or promiscuity which may be considered immoral. HIV infection is widely known to be incurable and people are afraid of contracting it. The link between sex and illness means that people who contract HIV are often thought to have brought it upon themselves as a result of personal irresponsibility or immorality. These factors combine to create a stigma around HIV which underpins prejudice, discrimination and even violence towards people infected. Negative attitudes to HIV are widely reinforced in media coverage of the issue and are prevalent in the general population.

Stigma means that some people do not seek HIV testing or may be reluctant to agree to an HIV test, despite knowing they might be at risk. Others do not consider HIV testing because they may not be aware that they could be infected, or they do not think that they belong to a group that is vulnerable to HIV, or they have little information or understanding about HIV transmission.

Despite the availability of effective treatment in the UK which has led to people with HIV becoming less easily identifiable, very few people with HIV feel able to be open about their HIV status. Few tell employers or colleagues at work, and many do not tell even their closest family and friends. Some people do not feel able to confide in their sexual partners or spouses for fear of rejection or abuse. The isolation and fear of being 'found out' and subsequently rejected or discriminated against, can be enormous, leading to stress and depression. In some communities, the stigma is so great that the HIV-negative members of those communities ostracise and reject the HIV-positive members.

Sometimes these fears are unfounded or exaggerated, and sharing with trusted family members and friends can provide great support. There are also voluntary and community organisations which provide support and services for people with HIV and these have helped many to cope with both the medical and social consequences of a positive HIV diagnosis.

People with HIV are now covered from the point of diagnosis by the provisions of the Disability Discrimination Act and this provides protection against discrimination in a variety of fields, including employment and the provision of goods, facilities and services. The Department of Health recognises that stigma is an important determining factor in the level of uptake of HIV testing[39] and has funded a number of interventions aimed a reducing the stigma surrounding HIV. One of these is the NAM publication *HIV, stigma and you*[40] which provides useful information on the nature and effects of HIV-related stigma.

Clinicians' concerns about HIV testing

HIV is a recent phenomenon. What we now understand as AIDS was only described in the medical literature in 1981. Historically, all aspects of HIV diagnosis, treatment and care have been managed within the specialties of GUM or Infectious Diseases. Because of this, the opportunities for generalists and other specialist clinicians to gain experience in diagnosing HIV, offering testing or understanding the concerns of people with HIV have been limited. This was, in part, a pragmatic response to the way in which HIV and AIDS were represented in the media in the early days of the epidemic which created a stigma around HIV infection, but this 'exceptional' approach to HIV has made clinicians hesitant about recommending HIV testing and has led to clinicians being deskilled. This has inadvertently perpetuated the secrecy, discrimination and stigma surrounding an HIV diagnosis. This section examines the common barrier that clinicians might encounter to offering HIV testing to patients.

Fear of embarrassing the patient

Some clinicians are reluctant to offer HIV testing to people from groups most at risk from HIV in situations where there are no overt signs of infection in case they are perceived as making a judgement about that person's sexual orientation, lifestyle or immigration status. Equally, when patients do not have obvious risks of infection this potential for embarrassment has prevented discussion of HIV where there are clinical signs of infection.

A useful rule of thumb is that an embarrassed doctor leads to an embarrassed patient so it is best to be open about the reasons for offering an HIV test. Where indicated by symptoms, simply state that when these

case study

Late diagnosis

Mr D, a 66-year-old married man was admitted to hospital with diarrhoea, weight loss, weakness and confusion. Over the preceding six months he had been admitted to hospital on two occasions with similar symptoms and investigated extensively for occult malignancy without a diagnosis being made and no HIV risk assessment was undertaken. On examination he was cachectic, disorientated and febrile, with a small pigmented lesion on his shin.

An HIV test proved positive and further investigations showed he had CMV encephalopathy, CMV retinitis and cutaneous Kaposi's sarcoma. His CD4 count was 60 cells/mm^3. Mr D made a full neurological recovery after receiving antiretroviral therapy.

Learning point

- If the symptoms could indicate HIV infection it is important to offer an HIV test even if a risk assessment has not been done.

symptoms are present, the recommendation is that an HIV test is carried out. Citing the authority of the *UK National Guidelines for HIV Testing 2008* and saying that this is part of good medical practice can help to reassure the patient that no judgements are being made about any aspect of their personal circumstances.

Lack of time

In many secondary care settings such as outpatient clinics, time can be at a premium and many clinicians fear being drawn into protracted discussions if they suggest an HIV test. Once again, a clear statement of the clinical reasoning for the offer is helpful here, and reassuring the patient about the confidentiality of the service and the lack of repercussions from a negative result can help to reduce anxiety.

Written information explaining the test is also helpful as it gives the patient and the clinician something to work through and provides a neat framework for the discussion.

Perceived lack of specialist HIV counselling skills

Talking about HIV should not be seen as 'special'. Clinicians are used to talking about sensitive issues and HIV should not be thought of differently. Some clinicians think that in-depth counselling is required prior to offering an HIV test. This is no longer the case and a short, focused pre-test discussion similar to that before any test which may result in a potentially life-altering diagnosis for a patient is recommended. Sections 4 and 5 on pre- and post-test discussion provide helpful approaches to discussing HIV with patients.

'The patient won't cope with a dual diagnosis'

Some clinicians worry that a patient will become depressed or suicidal if they find out that they have HIV, particularly if they are presenting with a

Men who have sex with men

Mr P, a 55-year-old man presented to a sexual health clinic asking for routine screening. He was originally from India, but had lived in the UK for most of his adult life. He was asymptomatic and gave a sexual history of a long-term female partner and a couple of casual female partners in the last few years. Men who attend sexual health clinics are routinely asked if they have ever had sex with men. He denied this.

He saw a nurse and had a routine screen for STIs, including an HIV test. The result was positive. When the health adviser gave Mr P the positive result at follow-up, he disclosed that he was gay, with a long-term male partner and a few casual male partners over the past few years. He attended for his initial appointment and the testing of partners was arranged. However Mr P was very concerned as he was well known in the local community with business interests locally. He decided to access HIV care in a different area, as anonymity was very important to him. This was facilitated for him by the clinic to ensure the appropriate handover of information.

Learning point
- Some men who have sex with men may initially not volunteer or be reluctant to disclose information about their sexual life.

serious condition and do not think that they are at risk from HIV. Although no patient welcomes a diagnosis, the situation for people with HIV in the UK is much more optimistic than it was 10 years ago, and it is important to emphasise that the first condition can only be effectively treated if the HIV is managed well.

'The patient doesn't consider themselves at risk'

Knowledge about HIV in the UK is deteriorating. In 2005 a survey conducted for the National AIDS Trust indicated that people in the UK knew less about HIV compared to five years previously[41]. The 2007 results of the same survey show that the trend is continuing[42]. Many people think that as HIV in the UK is largely confined to particular groups, such as 'gay men, drug users and people from Africa' they have no reason to consider themselves at risk.

Working with groups most at risk of HIV infection

HIV in the UK is most common in certain population groups:
- men who have sex with men
- people from sub-Saharan Africa or who have lived there
- injecting drug users.

Members of all these groups may already feel marginalised or stigmatised in UK society. The stigma and discrimination associated with HIV can exacerbate this.

Men who have sex with men

This term is used to describe both men who identify as gay, and also those who have sexual encounters with other men without considering themselves to be homosexual. While gay men may have a sense of belonging and access to gay-oriented culture, other men who have sex with men often see themselves as bisexual or even heterosexual, are sometimes married, and may not be willing to be open about their same-sex encounters.

African communities

Fear and prejudice against HIV is often very high in African communities, with resultant stigma and secrecy. Many people from high-prevalence countries will know of family members or friends who are living with, or have died from, HIV. This is particularly true for people from southern Africa as adult HIV prevalence rates are in the order of 15-25 per cent in countries like Zimbabwe, Zambia, Botswana and South Africa. In some families HIV may affect both parents and some of the children, creating major family needs.

When offering HIV testing to people from this group, it is essential to present information in a culturally sensitive way. Worries about employment and immigration and asylum issues can compound anxiety about confidentiality and disclosure of HIV status. The more medical aspects of HIV may be difficult for patients who do not have English as a first language, or come from countries such as conflict/post-conflict settings where they may have had limited opportunities for formal education.

case study

Cultural factors affect how a patient deals with their diagnosis

Mrs M was a 45-year-old Nigerian hairdresser/beautician. She was separated from her husband and had lived in the UK for five years with her three daughters. She presented with a severe bacterial pneumonia due to *Mycoplasma pneumoniae*, requiring hospital admission. On examination the doctor noticed that she had some scarring on her trunk compatible with previous herpes zoster. She made a good recovery from her pneumonia and the doctor suggested HIV testing, to which she agreed. The result was positive and her CD4 count was 190 cells/mm^3. She was referred to the HIV team who initiated ART, carefully explaining the regimen, potential side-effects and the need to adhere rigorously to her treatment. She was given information about a local support group for women with HIV and an appointment to see the HIV team in outpatients in two weeks time.

When she was seen in outpatients two months later, the repeat CD4 count was 160 cells/mm^3 and her viral load was still high. She admitted she had not been taking treatment because she had 'great faith in God and he is looking after her'. She had confided to a pastor at her church who had prayed with her and was confident that she would get better without treatment.

Learning point

- Some patients' religious and cultural beliefs will affect their understanding of HIV.

Cultural, social and religious views may also affect understanding of and beliefs about illness and treatment, so it is important to check patients' understanding of key issues, as many may not remember a great deal of what you have told them during the consultation. Cultural and religious beliefs may also affect how people will cope with a diagnosis of HIV. It is important to explore these beliefs as they may affect future treatment and adherence and to be open and non-judgmental when discussing these issues. It is often helpful to have patient leaflets available which cover key issues about HIV and give contact details of local support groups and HIV services.

case study

Injecting drug user

Mr Z, aged 29, originally from Spain but now living in the UK, presented in ED with a large groin abscess and evidence of recent injecting. He was thin, febrile and agitated. He was of no fixed abode and spoke little English. When an interpreter was found it was established that he had recently come to the UK following family problems and had been injecting drugs for many years. He denied ever having had an HIV test but agreed to undergo testing. The HIV test was positive, with a CD4 count of 220 cells/mm^3, a viral load of 15,000 copies/ml and hepatitis C antibody was detectable.

Learning point

- HIV and hepatitis C are common in people who inject drugs, especially in people who come from countries which have been slower to adopt safe injecting programmes.
- People diagnosed with HIV in any setting should be referred for specialist evaluation within two weeks according to the national Standards for HIV Clinical Care.
- Improved survival of patients with HIV means that hepatitis C co-infection should be actively sought and treated to prevent progression to cirrhosis and hepatocellular carcinoma.
- Co-infected patients should be referred to the HIV specialist team as soon as possible for assessment for ART regardless of their CD4 count and viral load.

Injecting drug users (IDUs)

Those who have acquired HIV through injecting drugs (even if they no longer use drugs) will be aware of being doubly stigmatised; as drug users they are a socially excluded group, and this may be compounded by a positive HIV status. Those who have not wished to access support, or who have been unable to, may be locked in a cycle of problems as they try to fund their drug use. Dependent drug use may restrict the ability to attend appointments or to take medication regularly. In some cases, HIV may not be a priority in comparison to the daily problems associated with drug dependence.

Patients with no obvious risk factors

Although HIV is statistically more likely to be found in people in the groups mentioned above, HIV can be seen in patients who have no obvious risk factors or who deny any HIV-associated risk behaviour. Some things that happened many years ago may have been forgotten, or the patient may be in denial about them. These could be an isolated episode of injecting drug use, receiving a blood transfusion or other invasive medical procedure in an area of high

case study

Patient with no obvious risk factors

Mrs G was 58 years old, overweight and alcohol dependent. She had been referred for assessment prior to admission for detoxification from alcohol abuse. Routine blood tests showed abnormal liver function tests, anaemia and neutropenia. Her doctor sent off further tests having obtained consent and was surprised when she was also found to have syphilis, hepatitis B and HIV. She had never injected drugs and had a long-term boyfriend. Her boyfriend had been on several golfing holidays in South Africa where, unbeknownst to her, he had had unprotected sex with commercial sex workers.

Learning points
- Some people have no obvious risk factors for HIV infection.
- People who think that they have no HIV risk factors may need specialist counselling and support to help them cope with a diagnosis.

HIV prevalence or having sexual contact with a person from an area of high HIV prevalence. Others may be genuinely unaware that they have been exposed to HIV.

While rare, such instances do occur and it is important to offer an HIV test where clinically indicated. The issues raised by such cases highlight the need to involve the HIV specialist team who can provide guidance on how to give a positive result sensitively and ensure that partner notification is dealt with appropriately.

case study

Patient suspects they might have HIV

Mrs M was a 27-year-old woman attending antenatal clinic for her first pregnancy. She was found to be HIV-positive during routine antenatal screening, and enrolled in a prevention-of-mother-to-child-transmission programme. She suspected that she might have acquired HIV from a previous boyfriend who injected drugs, but refused to tell her husband, because she said he would blame her and was likely to be violent towards her.

Learning points
- HIV stigma is so great in some communities that HIV-infected people may prefer to conceal their diagnosis from partners and family.
- Specialist HIV services are best placed to deal with the sensitive issues raised.

The patient may suspect that he/she has HIV, but may not volunteer information

Some people, particularly from groups where HIV is prevalent, are very aware of HIV and may have partners, friends or family who are living with HIV. It may be something that they often worry about, but which they are hesitant to mention, especially if they are attending medical services to which they do not consider HIV relevant, eg family planning or gynaecology clinics. Asking probing questions, such as, 'Is there anything particular that you have been worrying about?' or 'Is there anything that you think could be causing this problem?' and reassuring them of the confidentiality of your service may elicit anxieties about HIV.

SECTION 7

Annexes

IN THIS SECTION

Annexes

Annexe A: Advice on testing without consent

The situations in which you might consider testing a patient for HIV who lacks the capacity to consent are most likely to arise in inpatient situations eg where the patient has been admitted to the ICU or via the ED and is very ill, or in and out of consciousness. In England, the provisions of the Mental Capacity Act 2005[43] apply, and in Scotland this is covered by the Adults with Incapacity Act (Scotland) 2000[44]. In the first instance it is important to determine whether incapacity to consent to testing is temporary, fluctuating or permanent. Where incapacity is temporary, eg the patient is recovering from anaesthesia or under the influence of alcohol or drugs, you should wait until capacity is regained unless there is a compelling reason why this would not be in the patient's best interest. If capacity is fluctuating, eg in dementia, you should use a period of capacity to establish the patient's views on HIV testing and record these for review to establish that their views are consistent and can be relied on.

Testing without the patient's consent is only justified in rare circumstances, and if it will affect the immediate care of the patient. Guidance from the BMA on assessing capacity should be consulted if this is considered[45,46,47]. There are two main sets of circumstances under which testing without consent may need to be considered.

Patients without the mental capacity to consent

There may be cases when a patient is unable (eg due to severe depression or cognitive impairment) or unwilling (eg due to mania or psychosis) to give consent, but it is in his/her best interest to be tested in order to provide optimal medical care. When considering HIV testing without consent, the clinician must ensure that a clear reason for testing is established, and that testing is of specific benefit to the patient's clinical management.

The unconscious patient

The same principles should be taken into account when HIV testing is being considered

---

Testing the unconscious patient without consent[48]

Where a diagnosis of HIV would lead to a change in management of the patient's condition, the decision should be taken by the patient's consultant and should be discussed with the Infectious Diseases, Medical Microbiology or GUM teams.

- Document in the notes that the test is being done for direct patient care reasons
- There is no legal obligation to seek permission from the patient's relatives, or inform them that the test is being performed
- If tested for HIV, the patient should be informed of the result in confidence once they are sufficiently alert to understand and remember the result
- If positive, seek immediate advice from the specialist team.

---

in the unconscious patient. Whenever testing without consent is being explored, full consultation with the medical and/or mental health team and clear documentation of the rationale and decisions involved is recommended.

Annexe B: Post-exposure prophylaxis (PEP)

PEP for occupational exposure (needlestick injuries)

PEP is the emergency use of antiretroviral therapy (ART) to prevent transmission when a person has had a high risk exposure to HIV, eg following a needlestick injury where the source person is known to have HIV. It is important to act quickly as, if PEP is to be given, it should be given as soon as possible after the exposure (within hours) to maximise effectiveness. PEP is generally not recommended beyond 72 hours after exposure.

If the source patient is of unknown HIV status, it is recommended that they are tested urgently for HIV. The use of a rapid testing device (or point of care test) may be useful where obtaining a laboratory test result will be delayed. Informed consent must be obtained from the patient in this case, as for any other HIV test, and if the patient does not wish to know the result it is possible to test them without documenting the result in their notes.

PEP can be unpleasant to take as the drugs have side-effects. This needs to be balanced against the risk of transmission after a given type of exposure:

- 3/1000 for percutaneous exposure
- less than 1/1000 for mucocutaneous exposure.

Exposure of HIV-infected blood to intact skin is not considered to pose any risk of infection.

In any hospital setting there will be local arrangements for urgent advice about occupational exposure and PEP as well as agreed protocols, involving reference to appropriate specialists and out-of-hours cover arrangements. An initial risk assessment of the exposure incident should be made by the designated healthcare worker responsible for PEP, taking into account the nature of the exposure and the viral load of the source patient.

The exact choice of drug combination requires expert guidance. If there is information about the source patient's virus, this will influence the choice of PEP. DH guidelines should be consulted for the latest recommended PEP starter regimen[19]. The medication is usually taken for four weeks but can have significant side-effects. Because of the high risk of side-effects with PEP, many doctors routinely prescribe an anti-emetic such as cyclizine and an anti-diarrhoea drug such as lomotil.

Some people who have been prescribed ART prophylaxis report not taking the fully prescribed course, so counselling and adherence support should be available for the exposed healthcare worker.

The unconscious source patient in a needlestick injury

In the event of a needlestick injury or similar accident, it is illegal to test an unconscious source patient for HIV for the benefit of another individual, eg to reassure the exposed healthcare worker that they are not at risk of acquiring HIV, or to avoid taking potentially toxic post-exposure prophylaxis for four weeks. This is the subject of ongoing public debate, and a useful analysis of the issues can be found in a December 2007 editorial by White in the journal *Anaesthesia*[49].

Post-exposure prophylaxis following sexual exposure (PEPSE)

In the instance of a condom rupturing (or not being used), it is considered appropriate to offer PEPSE to the uninfected sexual partner of someone known to have HIV. PEPSE following potential sexual exposure to HIV is only recommended when the individual presents within 72 hours of exposure, and PEPSE should be given as early as possible within this timeframe. A course of PEPSE lasts four weeks.

PEPSE is available from HIV and GUM clinics and from emergency departments when these are closed. Anyone presenting for PEPSE needs to be assessed according to the BASHH UK guideline for the use of PEPSE[20] which states that:

'...a risk vs. benefit analysis should be undertaken for every individual presenting following an exposure and the decision to initiate PEP made on a case-by-case basis. This should consider both the risk of transmission according to the coital act and the risk of the source being HIV-positive. Consideration should be given to the possibility of the presenting individual having already been infected with HIV, and the ability to adhere to and tolerate the proposed antiretroviral drug regimen. The wishes of the individual should be considered at all times.'

PEPSE is recommended for receptive anal sex when the source individual is from a group or area of high prevalence, and for both receptive and insertive anal and vaginal sex if the source individual is known to be HIV-positive[20]. Where the HIV status of the source is unknown, PEPSE is considered for receptive anal sex, but not recommended for receptive vaginal sex.

PEPSE following sexual assault

PEPSE should also be considered following sexual assault, and police guidelines[50] recommend PEPSE for receptive vaginal and anal sex if the source individual is known to be HIV-positive. If the source is from an area of high prevalence (greater than 10%), PEPSE is recommended for receptive anal sex and considered for receptive vaginal sex. In line with the BASHH guideline, where the HIV status of the source is unknown, PEPSE is considered for receptive anal sex, but not recommended for receptive vaginal sex unless there is trauma or bleeding.

Annexe C: The patient diagnosed very late

The dying patient

The use of ART has meant that death as result of HIV infection has become much less common. Nevertheless, deaths still occur, and the secondary care team may be involved in decisions regarding care as death approaches. With ART it is harder to define when a patient is terminally ill because, given time, there can be recovery of immunity if ART is commenced or the regimen altered. However, until that happens the patient remains vulnerable to opportunistic infections. With this uncertainty about outcome, there is a need to integrate palliative and curative approaches to care, and the goals of HIV palliative care need to be redefined.

Involvement of other healthcare professionals

The course of advanced HIV disease may be more 'up and down' than other conditions requiring palliative care. Continuity and communication are extremely important in palliative care, and general practice, rather than secondary care, is often best-suited to providing these. The patient should be offered the support and involvement of palliative services and community nursing if appropriate. Some GPs can harness the support of specialist community nurses in HIV care. Hospice care may be needed. Respite care and symptom control are currently the most important indications for admission.

The following advice is taken from the GMC website's FAQ's section

Questions relating to the guidance on disclosure after a patient's death

(see paragraph 30 of *Confidentiality: Protecting and Providing Information 2004*)

Q18 Is it true that the duty of confidentiality continues after the patient's death?

Yes, but the extent to which information may be disclosed will depend on the circumstances. *Confidentiality: Protecting and Providing Information 2004* sets out criteria you need to consider. But there are circumstances in which you should disclose information, eg:

- to assist a Coroner, Procurator Fiscal or other similar officer with an inquest or fatal accident inquiry (see also paragraph 69 of *Good Medical Practice 2006*)
- to National Confidential Inquiries or other clinical audit or for education or research. Information should be anonymised wherever possible
- on death certificates. You must complete death certificates honestly and fully.

If a patient dies with HIV

The issue of death certification for people who have died of HIV-related illness can be complicated. It is commonly accepted that confidentiality persists after death and there are ethical considerations regarding such confidentiality when a patient or their relatives do not wish HIV to be recorded as a cause of death due to the stigma surrounding it. However, there is a clear legal requirement to indicate on the death certificate any underlying condition which may have contributed to a patient's death, and while this may potentially cause conflict with a patient's or their relatives' wishes the clinician's duty to comply with the law is clear and unambiguous.

Since the Shipman Enquiry, and with the rise in deaths from hospital acquired infections, it has become clear that this is an area which is under renewed scrutiny. Recently the English CMO emphasised this in a recent letter on healthcare associated infections and death certificates, reminding clinicians of the importance of complying with statutory requirements on death certification[51].

SECTION 8

Useful sources
of further information

Useful sources of further information

Websites for clinicians

British Association for Sexual Health and HIV (BASHH)
www.bashh.org
Professional organisation for GU medicine that produces sexually transmitted infections treatment guidelines.

British HIV Association (BHIVA)
www.bhiva.org
Regularly updated guidelines for treatment of HIV-infected adults with ART and associated guidelines (HIV in pregnancy, HIV and hepatitis co-infection, adherence support).

British Infection Society (BIS)
www.britishinfectionsociety.org
Wide ranging infection interests including HIV, hepatitis and opportunistic infections. Includes summary and links to guidelines of best infection practice and HIV-related guidelines produced jointly with BASHH, BHIVA and other groups

Children's HIV Association of the UK and Ireland (CHIVA)
www.chiva.org.uk
Contains articles and protocols on treatment and care of HIV-infected children and information on the Children's HIV National Network (CHINN).

Drug interactions
www.hiv-druginteractions.org
An HIV pharmacology resource for healthcare professionals and scientific researchers with the latest publications on drug interactions.

Health Protection Agency
www.hpa.org.uk
Up-to-date epidemiology figures for HIV and other infections in the UK, including graphs and slides that can be downloaded and CDR Weekly, an electronic epidemiological bulletin.

Websites for patients

AVERT (AIDS education and research)
www.avert.org
Abundant information on HIV-related education, prevention and care, including information for young people, statistics and information about transmission, treatment and testing.

NAM
www.aidsmap.com
A wealth of information on HIV and ART, including updates on the latest research findings.

HIV i-base
www.i-base.info
HIV information for healthcare professionals and HIV-positive people including information on I IIV treatment guidelines, answers to HIV treatment questions and materials for advocacy.

Patient plus
www.patient.co.uk/showdoc/40025264/
Information on HIV post-exposure prophylaxis which includes information on prescriptions, monitoring and follow-up.

Leaflets for patients

NAM Patient Information Booklets
Plain English information on key treatment topics and other HIV-related issues.
www.aidsmap.com/cms1187580.asp

HIV therapy NAM (2008)
Information for those considering starting antiretroviral therapy.
www.aidsmap.com/files/file1000889.pdf

HIV and TB NAM (2006)
Information on HIV/TB co-infection. Deals with treatments and drug interactions.
www.aidsmap.com/files/file1000888.pdf

HIV, stigma and you NAM (2006)
Information on how to deal with stigma and discrimination if it is encountered in everyday life.
www.aidsmap.com/files/file1001097.pdf

AIDS and HIV information AVERT (2007)
Basic information on a wide range of issues including HIV and AIDS help lines, guide to HIV testing, treatment, STIs, and pregnancy.
www.avert.org/help.htm

HIV: Looking after your sexual health fpa (2007)
An information leaflet about HIV and HIV testing for the general public.
www.fpa.org.uk/attachments/published/150/PDF%20HIV%20April%20 2007.pdf

Organisations for support and information
There may be local organisations accessible to you that are working with people with HIV. Below are listed just a few national organisations, which may provide you the means of identifying local ones:

Sexual health information line
0800 567 123 (calls may be charged from mobile phones)
24-hour, free, confidential helpline for anyone concerned about HIV or sexual health. Translation services are available and can provide details of local HIV organisations.

Terence Higgins Trust
www.tht.org.uk
A large charitable organisation with support services in many British towns and cities, THT produces a wide range of written resources on HIV prevention and living with HIV.
THT Direct helpline: 0845 1221 200
Monday to Friday 10am - 10pm, Saturday and Sunday 12 noon - 6pm.
http://www.tht.org.uk/howwecanhelpyou/needhelpnow/thtdirect/

Positively Women
www.positivelywomen.org.uk
020 7713 0222
Monday to Friday, 10am - 1pm and 2pm - 4pm
Women living with HIV answer the helpline and will ring back free of charge.
A registered charity which offers a range of peer support, advice, information and advocacy services for HIV-positive women.

African AIDS Helpline
www.blackhealthagency.org.uk/index.php/Section16.html
0800 0967 500
Monday to Friday (except bank holidays), 10am - 6pm (Answerphone
service available outside these hours).
Languages available: English, French, Portuguese, Luganda, Shona and
Swahili.

The Medical Foundation for the Care of Victims of Torture
www.torturecare.org.uk
The only organisation in the UK dedicated solely to the treatment of torture
survivors. It has four offices, in London, Manchester, Newcastle-upon-Tyne
and Glasgow.
See website for full contact and service details.

SECTION 9

REFERENCES:
HIV for non-HIV specialists

SECTION 9

References

1. Health Protection Agency, Centre for Infections. The UK Collaborative Group for HIV and STI Surveillance (2007) *Testing times. HIV and other sexually transmitted infections in the United Kingdom: 2007.* http://www.hpa.org.uk/web/HPAweb&HPAwebStandard/HPAweb_C/1203084355941

2. Health Protection Agency Centre for Infections (2008) New HIV Diagnoses: National Overview Web slides. http://www.hpa.org.uk/web/HPAwebFile/HPAweb_C/1219908756991 accessed 1 September 2008

3. Stöhr W, Dunn DT, Porter K et al on behalf of the UK CHIC Study (2007) CD4 cell count and initiation of antiretroviral therapy: trends in seven UK centres, 1997-2003. *HIV Medicine* **8**: 135-41.

4. Krentz HB, Auld MC & Gill MJ (2004) The high cost of medical care for patients who present late (CD4<200 cells/µL) with HIV infection. *HIV Medicine* **5**: 93-8.

5. British HIV Association (2006) *Clinical Audit Report 2005-6.* http://www.bhiva.org/files/file1030338.pdf

6. Sullivan AK, Curtis H, Sabin CA et al (2005). Newly diagnosed HIV infections: review in UK and Ireland. *BMJ* **330**: 1301-2. http://www.bmj.com/cgi/content/full/330/7503/1301

7. Sir Liam Donaldson, CMO & Christine Beasley, CNO (2007) *Improving the detection and diagnosis of HIV in non-HIV specialties including primary care.* 13 September 2007. http://www.info.doh.gov.uk/doh/embroadcast.nsf/vwDiscussionAll/EE0FA479BAA64A1B80257355003DFB47

8. Dr Harry Burns, CMO & Mr Paul Martin, CNO (2007) *Improving the detection and diagnosis of HIV in non-HIV specialties including primary care.* CEL 15. Chief Medical Officer and Chief Nursing Officer Directorates, Scottish Government. 23 October 2007.

9. Dr Tony Jewell, CMO & Rosemary Kennedy, CNO (2007) *Improving the detection and diagnosis of HIV in non-HIV specialties including primary care.* Department of Public Health and Health Professions, Welsh Assembly Government. 30 October 2007.

10. Dr Michael McBride, CMO & Mr Martin Bradley, CNO (2007) *Improving the detection and diagnosis of HIV in non-HIV specialties including primary care.* HSS(MD)23/2007. Department of Health, Social Services and Public Safety. 19 September 2007.

11. World Health Organization (WHO) and Joint United Nations Programme on AIDS (UNAIDS) (2007) *Guidance on provider-initiated HIV testing and counselling in health facilities.* Geneva: World Health Organization. http://whqlibdoc.who.int/publications/2007/9789241595568_eng.pdf

12. Centers for Disease Control and Prevention (2006) *Revised recommendations for HIV testing of adults, adolescents, and pregnant women in health-care settings. MMWR* **55/**(RR14): 1-17. http://www.cdc.gov/mmwr/preview/mmwrhtml/rr5514a1.htm

13. Department of Health (1996) *Guidelines for pre-test discussion on HIV testing.* http://www.dh.gov.uk/en/Publicationsandstatistics/Publications/PublicationsPolicyAndGuidance/DH_4005542

14. Marks G, Crepaz N & Janssen RS (2006) Estimating sexual transmission of HIV from persons aware and unaware that they are infected with the virus in the USA. *AIDS* **20**: 1447-50. http://www.aidsonline.com/pt/re/aids/pdfhandler.00002030-200606260-00012.pdf;jsessionid=LHGYMBT176T4KKms5qv9ynYGtQp7QnkvWryzQbJFB9jfm7v7Zz3v!1629792715!181195629!8091!-1

15. Vernazza P et al (2008) Les personnes séropositives ne souffrant d'aucune autre MST et suivant un traitement antirétroviral efficace ne transmettent pas le VIH par voie sexuelle (An HIV-infected person on antiretroviral therapy with completely suppressed viraemia ("effective ART") is not sexually infectious). *Bulletin des médecins suisses* **89**(5): 165-169. http://www.saez.ch/pdf_f/2008/2008-05/2008-05-089.PDF

16. Townsend C et al (2008) Low rates of mother-to-child transmission of HIV following effective pregnancy interventions in the United Kingdom and Ireland, 2000–2006. *AIDS* **22**: 973-81.

17. Department of Health (2002) *Good practice guidelines for renal dialysis/transplantation units: prevention and control of blood-borne virus infection.* http://www.dh.gov.uk/en/Publicationsandstatistics/Publications/PublicationsPolicyAndGuidance/DH_4005752

18. British HIV Association (2005) *Guidelines for kidney transplantation for patients with HIV disease.* Reviewed and endorsed by British Transplantation Society Standards Committee. http://www.bhiva.org/files/file1001320.pdf

19. Department of Health (2004) *HIV post-exposure prophylaxis: Guidance from the UK Chief Medical Officers' Expert Advisory Group on AIDS.* 2nd edition. http://www.dh.gov.uk/en/Publicationsandstatistics/Publications/PublicationsPolicyAndGuidance/DH_4083638

20. British Association for Sexual Health and HIV (2006) UK National Guideline for the use of post-exposure prophylaxis for HIV following sexual exposure. *Int J STD & AIDS* **17**: 81-92. http://www.bashh.org/documents/58/58.pdf

21. Joint United Nations Programme on HIV/AIDS (UNAIDS) website (2008) Latest Epidemiology Data. http://www.unaids.org/en/KnowledgeCentre/HIVData/Epidemiology/latestEpiData.asp accessed 1 September 2008

22. British Association for Sexual Health and HIV (2006) Clinical Governance Committee. *Guidance on the appropriate use of HIV Point of Care Tests.* http://www.bashh.org/committees/cgc/reports/final_hiv_point_of_care_tests_guidance_rev080606.pdf

23. British HIV Association, Royal College of Physicians, British Association for Sexual Health and HIV, British Infection Society (2007) *Standards for HIV clinical care.* http://www.bhiva.org/files/file1001299.pdf

24. British HIV Association (2008) *Guidelines for the management of HIV infection in pregnant women and the prevention of mother-to-child transmission of HIV. HIV Medicine* **9**: 452-502. http://www.bhiva.org/files/file1031055.pdf

25. Jones BE, Young SM, Antoniskis D et al (1993) Relationship of the manifestations of tuberculosis to CD4 cell counts in patients with human immunodeficiency virus infection. *Am Rev Respir Dis* **148**: 1292-7.

26. National Institute for Health and Clinical Excellence (2006) *CG33 Clinical diagnosis and management of tuberculosis, and measures for its prevention and control.* http://www.nice.org.uk/nicemedia/pdf/CG033niceguideline.pdf

27. Patel P et al (2008) Incidence of types of cancer among HIV-infected persons compared with the general population in the United States, 1992–2003. *Annals of Internal Medicine* **148**: 728-36.

28. Department of Health (2003) Screening for infectious diseases in pregnancy: standards to support the UK antenatal screening programme. London: Department of Health. http://www.dh.gov.uk/en/Publicationsandstatistics/Publications/PublicationsPolicyAndGuidance/DH_4050934

29. Sharland M, Blanche S, Castelli G et al for the PENTA Steering Committee (2004) PENTA guidelines for the use of antiretroviral therapy. *HIV Medicine* **5**(Suppl. 2): 61-86.

30. General Medical Council (2008) *Consent: patients and doctors making decisions together.* http://www.gmc-uk.org/news/index.asp#ConsentGuidance

31. General Medical Council (2004) *Confidentiality: protecting and providing information.* http://www.gmc-uk.org/guidance/current/library/confidentiality.asp

32. Association of British Insurers (1994) *ABI statement of practice – underwriting life insurance for HIV/AIDS.* http://www.abi.org.uk/Display/File/Child/197/HIV_SoBP_1994.doc

33. Association of British Insurers & British Medical Association (2008) *Medical information and insurance. Joint guidelines from the British Medical Association and the Association of British Insurers.* London: British Medical Association. http://www.bma.org.uk/ap.nsf/AttachmentsByTitle/PDFMedicalInfoInsurance/$FILE/MedicalInfoInsurance.pdf

34. Association of British Insurers (2004) *Statement of best practice on HIV and insurance* http://www.abi.org.uk/Display/File/86/HIV_SoBP_September_2004.doc

35. Bernard E, Azad Y, Geretti AM et al (2007) *HIV forensics: the use of phylogenetic analysis as evidence in criminal investigation of HIV transmission.* National AIDS Manual Briefing Papers. London: NAM. http://www.nat.org.uk/document/230

36. Crown Prosecution Service (2008) Policy for prosecuting cases involving the intentional or reckless sexual transmission of infectionhttp://www.cps.gov.uk/publications/prosecution/sti.htm

37. National AIDS Trust (2006) *Criminal Prosecution of HIV Transmission. NAT Policy Update.* http://www.nat.org.uk/document/185

38. Anderson J, Chalmers J, Nelson M et al (2006) *HIV transmission, the law and the work of the clinical team. A briefing paper.* http://www.bhiva.org/files/file1001327.pdf

39. Department of Health (2001) *Better prevention, better services, better sexual health – the national strategy for sexual health and HIV* London: Department of Health. http://www.dh.gov.uk/en/Publicationsandstatistics/Publications/PublicationsPolicyAndGuidance/DH_4003133

40. NAM (2006) *HIV, stigma and you.* London: NAM. http://www.aidsmap.com/files/file1001097.pdf

41. National AIDS Trust (2006) *Public attitudes HIV survey 2005.* London: National AIDS Trust. http://www.nat.org.uk/document/122.

42. National AIDS Trust (2008) *Public attitudes HIV survey 2007.* London: National AIDS Trust. http://www.nat.org.uk/document/405

43. Department for Constitutional Affairs (2007) *Mental Capacity Act 2005 code of practice.* London: TSO. http://www.dca.gov.uk/legal-policy/mental-capacity/mca-cp.pdf

44. Scottish Government (2007) *Revised codes of practice for the Adults with Incapacity Act.* http://www.scotland.gov.uk/Topics/Justice/Civil/awi/revisedcodes

45. British Medical Association (2007) *The Mental Capacity Act 2005 - Guidance for health professionals.* London: British Medical Association. http://www.bma.org.uk/ap.nsf/Content/mencapact05?OpenDocument&Highligh t=2,mental,capacity

46. British Medical Association and Law Society (2004) *Assessment of mental capacity: guidance for doctors and lawyers: 2nd edition.* London: BMJ Publications.

47. British Medical Association (2002) *Medical treatment for adults with incapacity: guidance on ethical and medico-legal issues in Scotland.* London: British Medical Association. http://www.bma.org.uk/ap.nsf/Content/AdultsincapacitySC

48. Iaegtmeyer M & Beeching N (2008) Practical approaches to HIV testing in the intensive care unit. *Journal of the Intensive Care Society* **9**: 37-41. http://journal.ics.ac.uk/pdf/0901037.pdf

49. White SM (2007) Needlestuck. *Anaesthesia.* **62**: 1199-201.

50. Home Office Police (2005). *Medical Care following Sexual Assault: Guidelines for Sexual Assault Referral Centres (SARCs).* http://police.homeoffice.gov.uk/publications/operational-policing/medical-care-sexual assault

51. Chief Medical Officer. PL CMO 2007(8) (2007) *Healthcare associated infections and death certification.* http://www.dh.gov.uk/en/Publicationsandstatistics/Lettersandcirculars/Professionalletters/Chiefmedicalofficerletters/DH_079104

SECTION 10

Subject index

Subject index

Notes: page numbers suffixed by 'f' indicate figures, 'i' indicate illustrations.

SECTION 10

SECTION 10

British Association for
Sexual Health and HIV (BASHH),
British HIV Association (BHIVA) and
British Infection Society (BIS)

UK National Guidelines for HIV Testing 2008

Executive summary

- HIV is now a treatable medical condition and the majority of those living with the virus remain fit and well on treatment.

- Despite this a significant number of people in the United Kingdom are unaware of their HIV infection and remain at risk to their own health and of passing their virus unwittingly on to others.

- Late diagnosis is the most important factor associated with HIV-related morbidity and mortality in the UK.

- Patients should therefore be offered and encouraged to accept HIV testing in a wider range of settings than is currently the case.

- Patients with specific indicator conditions should be routinely recommended to have an HIV test.

- All doctors, nurses and midwives should be able to obtain informed consent for an HIV test in the same way that they currently do for any other medical investigation.

Writing committee

British Association for Sexual Health and HIV (BASHH)	Adrian Palfreeman
British HIV Association (BHIVA)	Martin Fisher
British Infection Society (BIS)	Ed Ong
College of Emergency Medicine	James Wardrope
Royal College of General Practitioners	Ewen Stewart
Royal College of Nursing	Enrique Castro-Sanchez
Royal College of Physicians	Tim Peto, Karen Rogstad
Royal College of Paediatrics and Child Heath	Karen Rogstad
British Medical Association	Julian Sheather
Department of Health Expert Advisory Group on AIDS	Brian Gazzard, Deenan Pillay
General Medical Council	Jane O'Brien
Health Protection Agency	Valerie Delpech
Medical Foundation for AIDS & Sexual Health (MedFASH)	Ruth Lowbury, Russell Fleet
National AIDS Trust	Yusef Azad
Children's HIV Association (CHIVA)	Hermione Lyall
Society of Sexual Health Advisors	James Hardie
UK CAB	Godwin Adegbite
BASHH Clinical effectiveness group	Guy Rooney
Lay representative	Richard Whitehead

Contents

Introduction

These guidelines are intended to facilitate an increase in HIV testing in all healthcare settings as recommended by the UK's Chief Medical Officers and Chief Nursing Officers[1,2,3,4] in order to reduce the proportion of individuals with undiagnosed HIV infection with the aim of benefiting both individual and public health.

Misperceptions remain regarding HIV testing that hinder increased testing. In particular, many clinicians believe that lengthy pre-test counselling is required prior to testing. These guidelines provide the information needed to enable any clinician to perform an HIV test within good clinical practice and encourage 'normalisation' of HIV testing.

For this change in approach to be beneficial and ethically acceptable, it is imperative that following a positive HIV diagnosis, a newly diagnosed individual is immediately linked into appropriate HIV treatment and care.

This guidance refers to both diagnostic testing of individuals presenting with 'clinical indicator diseases' (ie where HIV infection enters the differential diagnosis) and opportunistic screening of populations where this is indicated on the basis of prevalence data. We also include an appendix on the provision of community-based HIV testing (Appendix 3).

It must be emphasised that in the UK, HIV testing remains voluntary and confidential. This is entirely possible within any healthcare setting if these guidelines are followed.

Background

Whilst the availability of highly active antiretroviral therapy (HAART) has transformed the outcome for individuals with HIV infection, there continues to be significant and avoidable morbidity and mortality relating to HIV infection in the UK.

A national audit by the British HIV Association (BHIVA) showed that of deaths occurring amongst HIV-positive adults in the UK in 2006, 24 per cent were directly attributable to the diagnosis of HIV being made too late for effective treatment[5]. Furthermore, it has been shown that many of these 'late presenters' have been seen in the recent past by healthcare professionals without the diagnosis having been made[6]. National surveillance data shows that approximately one-third of all HIV infections i adults in the UK remain undiagnosed[7] and that approximately 25 per cent of newly-diagnosed individuals have a CD4 count of less than 200 (an accepted marker of 'late' diagnosis).

Late diagnosis of HIV infection has been associated with increased mortality and morbidity[7], impaired response to HAART[8], and increased cost to healthcare services[9]. Furthermore, from a public health perspective, knowledge of HIV status is associated with a reduction in risk behaviour[10] and therefore it is anticipated that earlier diagnosis will result i reduced onward transmission[11]. Modelling has suggested that over 50 pe cent of new infections in the US occur through transmission from individuals in whom HIV has not been diagnosed. Furthermore, modelling in the US has also suggested that routine screening for HIV infection is cost effective and comparable to costs of other routinely offered screening where the prevalence of HIV exceeds 0.05 per cent[12].

All the published literature suggests that uptake of testing is increased where universal routine ('opt-out') strategies have been adopted [13,14,15].

Universal HIV ('opt-out') testing means that all individuals attending specified settings are offered and recommended an HIV test as part of routine care but an individual has the option to refuse a test.

Prior to 2001, HIV testing was largely confined to individuals presenting and requesting HIV testing in GUM clinics. The uptake of testing was low and a significant proportion of HIV-positive individuals were known to remain undiagnosed. The National Strategy for Sexual Health and HIV (2001)[16] recommended that all attendees at GUM clinics should be offered an HIV test with clear targets for the proportion offered testing and test uptake. Since this policy was introduced the proportion of infections which remain undiagnosed has reduced but still remains significant (25 per cent in heterosexuals, 47 per cent in men who have sex with men (MSM))[7]. The majority of GUM clinics now utilise a universal 'opt-out' approach to testing with high acceptability and success although the reasons why some high-risk individuals still refuse testing require further study.

In the antenatal setting, prior to 2000 uptake of HIV testing was highly variable and dependent upon healthcare worker factors rather than clinical need.

The only randomised controlled trial published to date[13] on testing methods showed that a universal 'opt–out' approach to HIV testing in antenatal patients was acceptable, did not cause anxiety and had a higher uptake than other methods. Assessing patients for risk merely reduced the number of patients tested and it is recognised that women who refuse antenatal testing are more likely to be HIV-positive.

The adoption of universal opt-out testing[17] has resulted in a dramatic improvement in antenatal testing rates and a significant reduction in the proportion of HIV infections that remain undiagnosed prior to delivery, from 18 per cent in 2000 to fewer than 10 per cent in 2006[7]. Furthermore the median CD4 count at HIV diagnosis of women detected through antenatal screening has been consistently higher than among other women (even after adjusting for age) and heterosexual men diagnosed with HIV. This indicates that efforts to detect HIV infection in asymptomatic individuals are likely to result in earlier diagnosis, hence reducing morbidity and mortality in diagnosed individuals as well as reducing onward transmission[7].

In the USA in 2006 the Centers for Disease Control and Prevention (CDC) recommended opt-out testing for all individuals aged 13 to 64 presenting to any healthcare facility (mainly Emergency Rooms) for any reason[18]. Initial reports suggest that this has been successful in increasing the number of new HIV diagnoses but barriers continue to exist including legal requirements in some states regarding testing, a requirement for written consent, and lack of access for some patients to ongoing HIV treatment and care[19].

In the UK, where the vast majority of patients have access to healthcare free at the point of delivery, all patients have access to a general practitioner and where there are pressures upon Emergency Departments to achieve four-hour waiting targets, we believe universal opt-out testing in all settings may not be the most feasible approach but support the use of opt-out testing in certain situations.

Confidentiality and HIV testing

HIV testing has historically been exceptionalised and treated differently to testing for other serious medical conditions. The outlook for individuals testing positive for HIV is now better than for many other serious illnesses for which clinicians routinely test.

Whilst there remains stigma associated with HIV infection, this can be minimised by following the general principles of confidentiality for any medical condition as laid down by the GMC in its guidance *Confidentiality protecting and providing information*[20].

'Patients have a right to expect that information about them will be held in confidence by their doctors. Confidentiality is central to trust between doctors and patients. Without assurances about confidentiality, patients may be reluctant to give doctors the information they need in order to provide good care.'

The result of an HIV test (if positive) should be given directly by the testing clinician (or team) to the patient and not via any third party, including relatives or other clinical teams unless the patient has specifically agreed to this (see section on post-test discussion).

Recommendations for testing

4.1 Who can test?
It should be within the competence of any doctor, midwife, nurse or trained healthcare worker to obtain consent for and conduct an HIV test.

4.2 Who should be offered a test?
A. Universal HIV testing is recommended in all of the following settings:
    1. GUM or sexual health clinics
    2. antenatal services
    3. termination of pregnancy services
    4. drug dependency programmes
    5. healthcare services for those diagnosed with tuberculosis, hepatitis B, hepatitis C and lymphoma.

B. An HIV test should be considered in the following settings where diagnosed HIV prevalence in the local population (PCT/LA) exceeds two in 1,000 population (see local PCT data[†])
    1. all men and women registering in general practice
    2. all general medical admissions.
The introduction of universal HIV testing in these settings should be thoroughly evaluated for acceptability and feasibility and the resultant data made available to better inform the ongoing implementation of this guideline.

C. HIV testing should be also routinely offered and recommended to the following patients:
    1. all patients presenting for healthcare where HIV, including primary HIV infection, enters the differential diagnosis (see table of indicator diseases and section on primary HIV infection)
    2. all patients diagnosed with a sexually transmitted infection
    3. all sexual partners of men and women known to be HIV-positive
    4. all men that have disclosed sexual contact with other men
    5. all female sexual contacts of men who have sex with men
    6. all patients reporting a history of injecting drug use
    7. all men and women known to be from a country of high HIV prevalence (>1 per cent*)
    8. all men and women who report sexual contact abroad or in the UK with individuals from countries of high HIV prevalence.*

*for an up to date list see http://www.unaids.org/en/KnowledgeCentre/
HIVData/Epidemiology/latestEpiData.asp

D. HIV testing should also be routinely performed in the following groups i
accordance with existing Department of Health guidance:
1. blood donors
2. dialysis patients
3. organ transplant donors and recipients.

4.3 How often to test?

Repeat testing should be provided for the following groups:
1. all individuals who have tested HIV-negative but where a possible
   exposure has occurred within the window period
2. men who have sex with men (MSM) – annually or more frequently if
   clinical symptoms are suggestive of seroconversion or ongoing high
   risk exposure
3. injecting drug users – annually or more frequently if clinical
   symptoms are suggestive of seroconversion (see section on primary
   HIV infection)
4. antenatal care – women who refuse an HIV test at booking should
   be re-offered a test and should they decline again an third offer of a
   test should be made at 36 weeks. Women presenting to services fo
   the first time in labour should be offered a point of care test (POCT).

A POCT test may also be considered for the infant of a woman who
refuses testing antenatally.

In areas of higher seroprevalence, or where there are other risk factors,
women who are HIV-negative at booking may be offered a routine second
test at 34-36 weeks' gestation as recommended in the BHIVA pregnancy
guidelines[21].

[†] Diagnosed prevalence is a good indicator of the undiagnosed prevalence in a population (ratio 2:1).
All PCTs are routinely informed of the diagnosed prevalence rate by the Health Protection Agency
(HPA) Survey of Prevalent HIV Diagnoses (SOPHID) data on an annual basis (further information on
SOPHID data and its dissemination is available at http://www.hpa.org.uk/web/
HPAweb&HPAwebStandard/HPAweb_C/1201767906579).
A diagnosed prevalence exceeding 2 in 1000, in those aged between 15 and 59, is a proxy for an
undiagnosed prevalence exceeding 1 in 1000, the threshold at which routine testing is assumed to I
cost effective based on the US data[18].

Table: Clinical indicator diseases for adult HIV infection

	AIDS-defining conditions	Other conditions where HIV testing should be offered
Respiratory	Tuberculosis Pneumocystis	Bacterial pneumonia Aspergillosis
Neurology	Cerebral toxoplasmosis Primary cerebral lymphoma Cryptococcal meningitis Progressive multifocal leucoencephalopathy	Aseptic meningitis/encephalitis Cerebral abscess Space occupying lesion of unknown cause Guillain-Barré Syndrome Transverse myelitis Peripheral neuropathy Dementia Leucoencephalopathy
Dermatology	Kaposi's sarcoma	Severe or recalcitrant seborrhoeic dermatitis Severe or recalcitrant psoriasis Multidermatomal or recurrent herpes zoster
Gastroenterology	Persistent cryptosporidiosis	Oral candidiasis Oral hairy leukoplakia Chronic diarrhoea of unknown cause Weight loss of unknown cause Salmonella, shigella or campylobacter Hepatitis B infection Hepatitis C infection
Oncology	Non-Hodgkin's lymphoma	Anal cancer or anal intraepithelial dysplasia Lung cancer Seminoma Head and neck cancer Hodgkin's lymphoma Castleman's disease
Gynaecology	Cervical cancer	Vaginal intraepithelial neoplasia Cervical intraepithelial neoplasia Grade 2 or above
Haematology		Any unexplained blood dyscrasia including: • thrombocytopenia • neutropenia • lymphopenia
Ophthalmology	Cytomegalovirus retinitis	Infective retinal diseases including herpesviruses and toxoplasma Any unexplained retinopathy
ENT		Lymphadenopathy of unknown cause Chronic parotitis Lymphoepithelial parotid cysts
Other		Mononucleosis-like syndrome (primary HIV infection) Pyrexia of unknown origin Any lymphadenopathy of unknown cause Any sexually transmitted infection

SECTION 4

Table: Clinical indicator diseases for paediatric HIV infection

	AIDS-defining conditions	Other conditions where HIV testing should be considered
ENT		Chronic parotitis, Recurrent and/or troublesome ear infections
Oral		Recurrent oral candidiasis Poor dental hygiene
Respiratory	Pneumocystis CMV pneumonitis Tuberculosis	Recurrent bacterial pneumonia Lymphoid interstitial pneumonitis Bronchiectasis
Neurology	HIV encephalopathy meningitis/encephalitis	Developmental delay Childhood stroke
Dermatology	Kaposi's sarcoma	Severe or recalcitrant dermatitis Multidermatomal or recurrent herpes zoster Recurrent fungal infections Extensive warts or molluscum contagiosum
Gastroenterology	Wasting syndrome Persistent cryptosporidiosis	Unexplained persistent hepatosplenomegaly Hepatitis B infection Hepatitis C infection
Oncology	Lymphoma Kaposi's sarcoma	
Haematology		Any unexplained blood dyscrasia including: • thrombocytopenia • neutropenia • lymphopenia
Ophthalmology	Cytomegalovirus retinitis	Any unexplained retinopathy
Other	Recurrent bacterial infections (eg meningitis, sepsis, osteomyelitis, pneumonia etc.) Pyrexia of unknown origin	

4.4 Which test to use?

There are two methods in routine practice for testing for HIV involving either venepuncture and a screening assay where blood is sent to a laboratory for testing or a rapid Point of Care Test (POCT).

Blood tests

The recommended first line assay is one which tests for HIV antibody AND p24 antigen simultaneously. These are termed fourth generation assays, and have the advantage of reducing the time between infection and testing HIV positive to one month which is one to two weeks earlier than with sensitive third generation (antibody only detection) assays[22]. It is reasonable to expect universal provision of these assays, although they are not offered by all primary screening laboratories.

HIV RNA quantitative assays (viral load tests) are not recommended as screening assays because of the possibility of false positive results, and also the only marginal advantage over fourth generation assays for detecting primary infection.

Confirmatory assays

Laboratories undertaking screening tests should be able to confirm antibody and antigen/RNA. There is a requirement for three independent assays, able to distinguish HIV-1 from HIV-2. These tests could be provided within the primary testing laboratory, or by a referral laboratory. All new HIV diagnoses should be made following appropriate confirmatory assays and testing a second sample.

Testing including confirmation should follow the standards laid out by the Health Protection Agency[23].

Point of care testing (POCT)

Point of care tests offer the advantage of a result from either a fingerprick or mouth swab sample within minutes. They have advantages of ease of use when venepuncture is not possible, eg outside conventional healthcare settings and where a delay in obtaining a result is a disadvantage, but these must be weighed against the disadvantages of a test which has reduced specificity and reduced sensitivity versus current fourth generation lab tests. Due to the low specificity of POCT and therefore the resulting poor positive predictive value all positive results must be confirmed by serological tests as there will be false positives, particularly in lower prevalence environments. Only CE-marked POCT kits should be used and a nominated accredited pathology laboratory should assist with governance issues and quality assurance of the testing process.

POCT is therefore recommended in the following contexts (see BASHH Point of Care Testing Guidance[24]):
1. clinical settings where a rapid turnaround of testing results is desirable
2. community testing sites

3. urgent source testing in cases of exposure incidents
4. circumstances in which venepuncture is refused.

General laboratory issues

All laboratories undertaking any diagnostic HIV services should be able to demonstrate satisfactory external quality control data for the tests undertaken, and should have full accreditation status[23] (such as clinical pathology accreditation (CPA)).

All laboratories must have satisfactory HIV diagnosis confirmatory assay systems available to allow timely definitive diagnoses. This may involve referring samples to specialist virology laboratories, if appropriate, or even national reference laboratories.

All acute healthcare settings should expect to have access to an urgent HIV screening assay result ideally within eight hours, and definitely within 24 hours, to provide optimal support for exposure incidents.

Routine opt-out test results should be expected to be available within 72 hours.

Pre-test discussion

The primary purpose of pre-test discussion is to establish informed consent for HIV testing. Lengthy pre-test HIV counselling is not a requirement, unless a patient requests or needs this[1,2,3,4].

The essential elements that the pre-test discussion should cover are:
- the benefits of testing to the individual
- details of how the result will be given.

This approach has been successful in GU and antenatal clinics and is generally acceptable.

For some patients raising the issue of HIV testing in other scenarios might require more explanation as to why the doctor or nurse is recommending this, for example when a patient presents with a condition which is more common in HIV infection.

As with any other medical investigation the discussion should address any other issues which may be raised by the patient as it is important that patients are given the opportunity to make a decision with adequate information about the test and the virus.

If a patient refuses a test the reasons why they have made that choice should be explored to ensure that these are not due to incorrect beliefs about the virus or the consequences of testing. If implications for either insurance or criminal prosecution for transmission are raised by the individual as reasons for not testing these should be further explored and any factual inaccuracies corrected (see Appendices 6 and 7).

Some patients may need additional help to make a decision, for example, because English is not their first language. It is essential to ensure that these patients have understood what is proposed, and why. It is also important to establish that the patient understands what a positive and a negative result mean in terms of infection with HIV as some patients could interpret 'positive' as good news.

Children and young people, and those with learning difficulties or mental health problems, may need additional support and time to understand what is proposed and to make a decision (see Appendices 3 and 4).

As with any other investigation the offer of an HIV test should be documented in the patient's case record together with any relevant discussion. If the patient refuses a test the reasons for this should be documented. Usually, written consent is unnecessary and may discourage HIV testing by exceptionalising it.

This advice is consistent with the GMC Guidance *Consent: patients and doctors making decisions together*[25].

Post-test discussion

As with any medical investigation it is essential that clear procedures are established as to how the patient will receive the result, with particular attention paid to the means by which a positive result will be delivered.

Arrangements for communicating the results should always be discussed and agreed with the patient at the time of testing, particularly if the test is being performed in an outpatient or emergency care setting.

Face-to-face provision of HIV test results is strongly encouraged for:
- ward-based patients
- patients more likely to have an HIV-positive result
- those with mental health issues or risk of suicide
- those for whom English is a second language
- young people under 16 years
- those who may be highly anxious or vulnerable.

Post-test discussion for individuals who test HIV-negative
It is considered good practice to offer health promotion screening for sexually transmitted infections and advice around risk reduction or behaviour change including discussion relating to post-exposure prophylaxis (PEP) to those individuals at higher risk of repeat exposure to HIV infection. This is best achieved by onward referral to GUM or HIV services or voluntary sector agencies.

The need for a repeat HIV test if still within the window period after a specific exposure should be discussed. Although fourth generation tests shorten the time from exposure to seroconversion a repeat test at three months is still recommended to definitively exclude HIV infection.

Occasionally HIV results are reported as reactive or equivocal. These patients may be sero-converting (see section on primary HIV infection) and management of re-testing may be complex and so such individuals should be promptly referred to specialist care.

Post-test discussion for individuals who test HIV-positive
As is good clinical practice for any situation where bad news is being conveyed, the result should be given face to face in a confidential environment and in a clear and direct manner. If a patient's first language is not English, consideration should be given to utilisation of an appropriate confidential translation service.

If a positive result is being given by a non-GUM/HIV specialist, it is essential, prior to giving the result, to have clarified knowledge of local specialist services and have established a clear pathway for onward referral.

It is recommended that any individual testing HIV-positive for the first time is seen by a specialist (HIV clinician, specialist nurse or sexual health adviser or voluntary sector counsellor) at the earliest possible opportunity preferably within 48 hours and certainly within two weeks of receiving the result[26].

More detailed post-test discussion (including assessment of disease stage, consideration of treatment, and partner notification) will be performed by the GUM/HIV specialist team.

Non-attendance for positive results

It is recommended to have an agreed recall process following failure of a patient to return for a positive result as with any other medical condition.

As with all other medical investigations it is the responsibility of the healthcare professional requesting the test to ensure that all results of investigations requested are received and acted upon where necessary.

If there is no means of contacting the patient or if attempts are unsuccessful, it is recommended that advice be sought from the local GUM/HIV team who are likely to have experience and resources to deal with this issue.

Suspected primary HIV infection

Primary HIV infection (PHI) or seroconversion illness occurs in approximately 80 per cent of individuals, typically two to four weeks after infection. It is well recognised that this represents a unique opportunity to prevent onward transmission as an individual is considerably more infectious at this stage. Furthermore this may be the only clinical opportunity to detect HIV before advanced immunosuppression many years later.

It is known that the features of PHI are non-specific, that individuals usually do present to medical services (primary or emergency care) but frequently the diagnosis is missed or not suspected.

The typical symptoms include a combination of any of:

- fever
- rash (maculopapular)
- myalgia
- pharyngitis
- headache/aseptic meningitis.

These resolve spontaneously within two to three weeks and therefore if PHI is suspected, this needs to be investigated at the time of presentation and not deferred.

It is recommended that consideration be given to HIV testing in any person with these symptoms perceived to be at risk of infection. It is acknowledged that in some non-GUM settings details of an individual's sexual risk may be difficult to ascertain, but a low threshold for offering a test should remain.

Although with fourth generation tests infection can be detected much earlier than previously (see section on primary screening assays), in very recent infection – when patients may be most symptomatic – the test may be negative. In this scenario, if PHI is suspected, either urgent referral to specialist services (GU Clinic or HIV service) or a repeat test in seven days is recommended. HIV viral load testing can be used in this clinical setting, but it is recommended that this is only performed with specialist input.

Appendices

Appendix 1. Providing written confirmation of results

There may be occasions when patients request or require written confirmation of their results.

A written protocol is recommended to set out criteria for those who receive results in this way and how this is done.

Clinicians who are not personally acquainted with the patient requesting such a letter should consider referring the patient back to their general practitioner.

If the patient requests a letter confirming their HIV status then ensure that they are correctly identified both at the time blood is taken and when the result is given, by documenting the method of identification such as photographic ID (eg passport, driving licence) in both the notes and the correspondence.

It is preferable to have a written letter signed by the doctor (or another appropriate healthcare professional), rather than a copy of the actual result, and this should be addressed to a specific individual, not 'To whom it may concern'.

Appendix 2. Detailed post-test discussion and partner notification

The following issues would normally be dealt with when the patient is seen at the HIV clinic.

Post-test discussion for individuals who test HIV-positive provides an opportunity to address any immediate concerns and to look at the individual's support and information needs.

It is good practice to check if the patient has any immediate medical problems. In case of any symptoms an immediate link with a doctor or nurse may be indicated.

It is again good practice to offer follow-up appointments (including testing where relevant) and ongoing support for the patient, partner or family where appropriate although this may be done by specialist GUM/HIV services.

Consideration should be given to discussion of partner notification. This will be dependent on the individual but services should have clear guidelines on partner notification in HIV, how it is offered, including offering clients the option of provider referral.

Issues such as preventing the onward transmission of HIV and the medico-legal issues surrounding this, as well as post-exposure prophylaxis for current or future partners who may be at risk, should also be discussed.

Appendix 3. Community-based HIV testing

Historically HIV testing has been performed almost exclusively in medical settings. More recently, programmes have been explored to evaluate testing in community settings. Such programmes acknowledge that many individuals may prefer to test in non-medical settings, may not be registered with primary care, may feel stigmatised by attending medical settings and being targeted for HIV testing, and may not be prepared to disclose risk behaviour, including sexual orientation, to healthcare professionals. The ability to perform community-based testing has been largely enabled by the development of newer technologies for HIV testing, particularly POCT (see section on point of care testing).

Pilot studies have shown that community-based testing is acceptable and feasible and may encourage potentially high-risk individuals who would not otherwise have accessed HIV testing through conventional services[27]. The development of such services, complementary to expansion of existing healthcare based services, should therefore be encouraged and evaluated, particularly in areas where there is a high prevalence of undiagnosed infection. It is vital to ensure that community testing services are linked to the local HIV clinic to ensure that patients will promptly and appropriately access care with clear referral pathways.

Potential disadvantages to community testing include the limitations of the current POCT technologies, such that very recent infection may be missed, and the higher rates of 'false positive' results compared to conventional laboratory-based testing. It is essential that anyone performing HIV testing in a non-healthcare setting has adequate governance arrangements including quality assurance.

The false positive rate will particularly affect individuals whose risk of HIV infection is low, and therefore it is recommended that such programmes are targeted toward communities where undiagnosed HIV prevalence is high, particularly MSM and immigrant communities.

If individuals report high risk activity within the 'window period' of POCTs (currently 12 weeks), either repeat testing in 12 weeks or attendance at a local healthcare HIV testing site should be encouraged.

Individuals who test negative for HIV but who are at risk of other sexually transmitted infections (particularly MSM) should be encouraged to attend local GUM services for testing for other infection and to ensure adequate immunisation against hepatitis viruses.

Appendix 4. Testing where the patient lacks capacity to consent (including the unconscious patient)

Legislation in England, Wales and Scotland provides a framework for decision making on behalf of adults aged 16 and over who lack capacity to make decisions on their own behalf. The Mental Capacity Act 2005 applies to England and Wales. In Scotland the Adults with Incapacity (Scotland) Act 2000 applies, for which there is a separate BMA guidance note. In Northern Ireland common law applies.

A person lacks capacity if, at the time the decision needs to be made, he or she is unable to make a decision because of a mental disorder, or is unable to communicate their decision. Key points to consider when assessing capacity:

1. the assessment of capacity relates to the specific issue in question – in this case consent to HIV testing
2. start from the presumption that the patient has capacity to make this decision
3. consider whether the patient understands what decision they are being asked to make and can weigh up the information relevant to the decision; do they understand the consequences of making a choice?
4. take all possible steps to help patients make a decision for themselves (eg provide information in a more accessible form – drawings, tapes etc). If you judge that a patient lacks capacity to consent to an HIV test you should consider whether this is temporary or permanent. If temporary, you should defer testing until the patient regains capacity, unless testing is immediately necessary to save the patient's life or prevent a serious deterioration of their condition.

If the lack of capacity is, or is likely to be, permanent you should seek a decision from any person with relevant powers of attorney or follow the requirements of any valid advance statements. If the patient has not appointed an attorney nor left a valid advance statement, HIV testing may be undertaken where this is in the best interests of the patient (England and Wales) or is necessary and of benefit to the patient (Scotland).

Guidance on assessing capacity is published by the BMA[28,29,30]. Advice on how to assess appropriate treatment of patients who lack capacity is available in the in the relevant statutory codes of practice for England[31] and Scotland[32].

If consciousness is regained the patient should be told of the test result as soon as practicable.

If they die, a decision should be made on disclosure according to the circumstances, eg others at risk and previously disclosed wishes.

Appendix 5. Testing infants, children and young people

Any infant/child/young person thought to be at significant risk of HIV infection, including all those with parents or siblings, who are HIV-infected, should be tested. It is in the best interest of the infant/child/ young person to be tested in these circumstances although this only needs to be undertaken urgently in infants who are at risk of rapid disease progression.

Who to consider HIV testing

- infants and children what ever their age where the mother has HIV, or may have died of an HIV-associated condition
- infants born to mothers known to have HIV in pregnancy
- infants born to mothers who have refused an HIV test in pregnancy
- infants and children who are presented for fostering/adoption where there is any risk of blood borne infections[33]
- infants and children newly arrived in the UK from high prevalence areas (they may be unaccompanied minors)
- infants and children with signs and symptoms consistent with an HIV diagnosis
- infants and children being screened for a congenital immunodeficiency
- infants and children in circumstances of post-exposure prophylaxis[34]
- infants and children in cases where there has been sexual abuse (see below).

Obtaining consent for HIV testing from children

In England and Wales, children are defined as those under 18 years old (Children Act 1989) and in Scotland as under 16 (Children (Scotland) Act 1995).

Under English law young people aged 16 years or over are assumed to have the capacity to consent to medical treatment and should be treated in the same way as adults.

Young people under 16 years accessing sexual healthcare (which would include HIV testing as part of a sexual health screen) without a parent or guardian should be assessed for competency to consent[35].

Testing in a non-competent child

If a child lacks the capacity to consent, then the consent of one parent or carer with parental responsibility is sufficient. If you are aware of parental disagreement, refer to GMC guidance[36].

Refusal of testing by a competent young person

This is a difficult area and varies according to country in the UK.

In Scotland, parents cannot override a refusal to test by a competent young person.

In England, Wales and Northern Ireland, the law on parents overriding a competent young person's refusal to testing is complex. Legal advice should be sought about whether to apply to the court if testing is thought to be in the best interests of a competent child who refuses.

Refusal of testing by parents of a non-competent child or young person

If parents refuse testing that is clearly in the best interests of a non-competen child or young person then you should consider involving other members of the multidisciplinary team, an independent advocate or named/designated doctor for child protection before seeking legal advice. This also applies if both a young person with capacity and their parents refuse testing.

Testing victims of child sexual abuse

Testing of victims of child sexual abuse should be considered in every case according to risk factors[36]. Testing should always be performed if post-exposure prophylaxis is to be given. Where parental consent is refused, refer to consent section of RCPCH guidelines on physical signs of child sexual abuse[37].

Testing of children of known HIV-positive parents

Testing should be offered in all cases at risk of vertical transmission. Increasing evidence shows that children infected vertically can be surviving into teenage years without being diagnosed. Therefore it can not be assumed that older children of mothers with HIV do not require testing. This raises difficult issues of informed consent for these young people, particularly if they are unaware of the mother's diagnosis.

Testing of neonates, children and young people where the mother refuses consent and/or disclosure of her HIV status is a complex area. The overriding consideration must be the best interests of the child, and multidisciplinary decision making and expert advice should be sought, including legal advice where appropriate. A mother's refusal is not acceptable. Referral to a paediatric centre with experience of management of HIV-infected children is strongly recommended.

Parents may need to be supported in making the decision to go ahead to test their children: paediatric HIV support is available nationally through the Children's HIV National Network (CHINN) details of which can be found on the Children's HIV Association (CHIVA) website: www.chiva.org.uk.

What do children need to know about having an HIV test?

One of the main reasons that parents do not want to test their children for HIV is because they are afraid to share the diagnosis with them. It should be explained to parents that a developmentally and age appropriate explanation of the test should be given to children and that this does not necessarily mean using the term HIV

1. Older children (usually those older than 11-12 years) should be asked to give consent for an HIV test.
2. Younger children (usually five to ten years of age) can be told they are being tested for a 'bug' in the blood,
3. Pre-school children and infants do not need any formal explanation of why they are having a blood test

Appropriate HIV tests for infants and children

Children older than 18 months of age: HIV antibody test, as for adults. Infants younger than 18 months of age: infants born to mothers with HIV receive transplacental maternal HIV antibodies which can usually be detected in the infant blood until about 18 months of age. Infants are therefore tested for genomic evidence of HIV by PCR. For details see BHIVA guidelines on the management of HIV in pregnancy[21].

Appendix 6. The source patient in a needlestick injury or other HIV risk exposure

The Human Tissue Act (2004) which governs the obtaining of source patient consent supersedes previous GMC guidance.

The source patient's consent to testing must always be gained. Consent from the patient should be obtained from a healthcare worker other than that who sustained the injury. If the rationale for testing is explained, it is unusual for consent to be refused. If the patient does not wish to know the result the option of testing without any documentation should be considered.

For guidance on testing a source patient from a needlestick injury who is unconscious or unable to give consent seek expert advice as the law on this is being reviewed. Guidance on Post-exposure prophylaxis for occupational exposure to HIV is published by the UK CMOs' Expert Advisory Group on AIDS (EAGA)[38].

Appendix 7. HIV testing and insurance

The ABI code of practice 1994 states that questions regarding whether an individual has ever had an HIV test or a negative result should not be asked. Applicants should however declare any positive results if asked as would be the case with any other medical condition[39,40].

Appendix 8. HIV testing and criminal prosecution for HIV transmission

Concern about this issue should not be a barrier to testing. There have been a number of prosecutions of individuals under the Offences Against the Person Act 1861 for reckless HIV transmission. This has included a prosecution of an individual who had not been HIV tested There is detailed guidance on the legal implications of this available from the voluntary sector as well as advice on safer sexual practices designed to minimise risk of transmission of HIV to others[41,42].

Appendix 9. Auditable standards

Standard	Audited by what data and by whom?	How often?	Comments
Offer and uptake of HIV test in GUM	GUMCAD; HPA	Annually	National report; local feedback
Offer and uptake in of HIV test in antenatal care	National Antenatal Infections Screening Monitoring programme (NAISM); HPA	Annually	National report; local feedback
Offer and uptake of HIV test in drug misuse services	Sentinel unlinked anonymous seroprevalence data, HPA	Annually	National report
Offer and uptake of HIV test in TOP services	Local clinic data sources	Annually	National report; local team discussion
Proportion of HIV undiagnosed (by risk group)	Sentinel unlinked anonymous seroprevalence data, HPA	Annually	National report
Proportion of newly diagnosed HIV-positive with CD4 < 200	New diagnoses/SOPHID/CD4 surveillance; HPA	Annually	National report; local feedback
Proportion of newly diagnosed HIV-positive with CD4 < 350	New diagnoses/SOPHID/CD4 surveillance; HPA	Annually	National report; local feedback
Number of HIV tests performed in primary care	Local lab with GUM/HIV/ID input	Annually	Local meeting with PCT if no increase
Number of HIV tests performed in secondary care	Local lab with GUM/HIV/ID input	Annually	Local meeting with relevant teams if no increase
Proportion of individuals with indicator disease being tested for HIV	Local data sources (using IT or case note audits)	Annually	Local team discussion
Offer and uptake of HIV test among TB patients	Chest/ID clinic (using IT or case note audits)	Annually	Joint meeting to discuss
Offer and uptake of HIV test among lymphoma patients	Oncology (using IT or case note audits)	Annually	Joint meeting to discuss
Offer and uptake of HIV test among hepatitis B and C patients	Hepatology/ID/gastroenterology(using IT or case note audits)	Annually	Joint meeting to discuss

Acknowledgements

The authors would like to thank all those listed below who responded to the consultation on these guidelines, which attracted a great deal of constructive and helpful comment much which has been incorporated into the final draft.

It has not however been possible to accommodate all of the suggestions and advice received as correspondents were divided in their approach to some of the issues. We have therefore made all of the feedback comment to the original consultation draft available on the BHIVA website www.bhiva.org.

The Terence Higgins Trust
The National Aids Trust
HIV Scotland
Sigma Research
African HIV Policy Network
Positively Women
GMFA
POZFEM
George House Trust
Waverley Care
Royal College of Paediatrics and Child Health
Association of Medical Microbiologists
Children's HIV Association
Professor Jackie Cassell
Professor Sebastian Lucas
Dr Alastair Miller
Dr Mary Poulton
Dr Andrew Winter

Dr C Mitsides
Dr Helen Lacey
Dr Ann Sullivan
Dr John White
Dr Clive Taylor
Dr Stephen Dawson
Dr Rudiger Pittrof
Dr Frances Sanderson
Dr John Parry
Roger Pebody
Christine Hardwick
Babs Evans
Gus Cairns
Hilary Curtis
Claire Blackstock
Kevin Miles
Kavita Dass
Max Courtney
Bev Ibbetson
Janet Murat and Sascha Auweiler

References

1. Sir Liam Donaldson, CMO & Christine Beasley, CNO. Improving the detection and diagnosis of HIV in non-HIV specialties including primary care. 13 September 2007. http://www.info.doh.gov.uk/doh/embroadcast.nsf/vwDiscussionAll/EE0FA479BAA64A1B80257355003DFB47

2. Dr Harry Burns, CMO & Mr Paul Martin, CNO. Improving the detection and diagnosis of HIV in non-HIV specialties including primary care. CEL 15. Chief Medical Officer and Chief Nursing Officer Directorates, Scottish Government. 23 October 2007.

3. Dr Tony Jewell, CMO & Rosemary Kennedy, CNO. Improving the detection and diagnosis of HIV in non-HIV specialties including primary care. Department of Public Health and Health Professions, Welsh Assembly Government. 30 October 2007.

4. Dr Michael McBride, CMO and Mr Martin Bradley, CNO. Improving the detection and diagnosis of HIV in non-HIV specialties including primary care. HSS(MD)23/2007. Department of Health, Social Services and Public Safety of Northern Ireland. 19 September 2007.

5. British HIV Association (BHIVA). 2005-6 mortality audit. http://www.bhiva.org/files/file1001379.ppt

6. Sullivan AK, Curtis H, Sabin CA et al (2005) Newly diagnosed HIV infections: review in UK and Ireland. *BMJ* **330**: 1301-2. http://www.bmj.com/cgi/content/full/330/7503/1301

7. Health Protection Agency (HPA), Centre for Infections. The UK Collaborative Group for HIV and STI Surveillance (2007) *Testing Times. HIV and other sexually transmitted infections in the United Kingdom: 2007.* http://www.hpa.org.uk/web/HPAweb&HPAwebStandard/HPAweb_C/1203084355941

8. Stöhr W, Dunn DT, Porter K et al (2007) on behalf of the UK CHIC Study. CD4 cell count and initiation of antiretroviral therapy: trends in seven UK centres, 1997-2003. *HIV Medicine* **8**:135–41.

9. Krentz HB, Auld MC & Gill MJ (2004) The high cost of medical care for patients who present late (CD4<200 cells/µL) with HIV infection. *HIV Medicine* **5**: 93-8.

10. Marks G, Crepaz N & Janssen RS (2006) Estimating sexual transmission of HIV from persons aware and unaware that they are infected with the virus in the USA. *AIDS* **20**: 1447-50. http://www.aidsonline.com/pt/re/aids/pdfhandler.00002030-200606260-00012.pdf;jsessionid=LHGYMBT176T4KKms5qv9ynYGtQp7QnkvWryzQhJFB9jfm7v7Zz3v!1629792715!181195629!8091!-1

11. Vernazza P, Hirschel B, Bernasconi E et al (2008) Les personnes séropositives ne souffrant d'aucune autre MST et suivant un traitement antirétroviral efficace ne transmettent pas le VIH par voie sexuelle (An HIV-infected person on antiretroviral therapy with completely suppressed viraemia ("effective ART") is not sexually infectious). *Bulletin des médecins suisses* **89**(5): 165-169. http://www.saez.ch/pdf_f/2008/2008-05/2008-05-089.PDF

12. Sanders GD, Bayoumi AM, Sundaram V et al (2005) Cost-Effectiveness of Screening for HIV in the Era of Highly Active Antiretroviral Therapy. *New Engl J Med* **352**: 570-85.

13. Simpson WM, Johnstone FD, Boyd FM et al (1998) Uptake and acceptability of antenatal HIV testing: randomised controlled trial of different methods of offering the test. *BMJ* **316**: 262–7.

14.Haukoos J, Hopkins E, Byyny R et al and The Denver Emergency Department HIV Testing Study Group (2008) Opt-out Rapid HIV Screening in the Emergency Department: Preliminary Results from a Prospective Clinical Trial. CROI 2008; abstract 544b. http://www.retroconference.org/2008/PDFs/544b.pdf

15. Cohan D, Gomez E & Charlebois E (2008) Patient Perspectives and Testing Uptake with Abbreviated versus Standard Pre-test HIV Counseling in the Prenatal Setting: A Randomized-Controlled, Non-inferiority Trial. CROI 2008; abstract 535a. http://www.retroconference.org/2008/PDFs/535a.pdf

16. Department of Health (DH) (2001) Better prevention, better services, better sexual health – the national strategy for sexual health and HIV. http://www.dh.gov. uk/en/Publicationsandstatistics/Publications/ PublicationsPolicyAndGuidance/DH_4003133

17. Department of Health (2003) Screening for infectious diseases in pregnancy. http://www.dh.gov. uk/en/Publicationsandstatistics/Publications/ PublicationsPolicyAndGuidance/DH_4050934

18. Centers for Disease Control and Prevention (CDC) (2006) Revised recommendations for HIV testing of adults, adolescents, and pregnant women in health-care settings. MMWR 55/(RR14): 1-17. http://www. cdc.gov/mmwr/preview/mmwrhtml/rr5514a1.htm

19. Walensky RP, Losina E, Malatesta L et al (2008) The high yield of routine HIV screening in urgent care sites in Massachusetts. CROI 2008; abstract 39.http://www. retroconference.org/2003/cd/Abstract/39.htm

20. General Medical Council (GMC) (2004) Confidentiality: protecting and providing information. http://www.gmc-uk.org/guidance/current/library/ confidentiality.asp

21. British HIV Association (2008) Guidelines for the management of HIV infection in pregnant women and the prevention of mother-to-child transmission of HIV HIV Medicine 9: 452-502. http://www.bhiva.org/files/file1031055.pdf

22. Barbara J, Ramskill S, Perry K et al (2006) The National Blood Service (England). Approach to evaluation of kits for detecting infectious agents. Transfusion Medicine Reviews 21: 147-58.

23. Health Protection Agency (2007) Anti-HIV screenin – minimum testing algorithm. National Standard Meth VSOP 11(1). http://www.hpa-standardmethods.org.uk/ documents/vsop/pdf/vsop11.pdf

24. British Association for Sexual Health and HIV (BASHH) (2006) Clinical Governance Committee. Guidance on the appropriate use of HIV Point of Care Tests. . http://www.bashh.org/committees/cgc/ reports/final_hiv_point_of_care_tests_guidance_ rev080606.pdf

25. General Medical Council (2008) Consent: patient and doctors making decisions together. http://www. gmc-uk.org/news/index.asp#ConsentGuidance

26. British HIV Association, Royal College of Physicia (RCP), British Association for Sexual Health and HIV, British Infection Society (BIS) (2007) Standards for H clinical care. http://www.bhiva.org/files/file1001299.pdf

27. Weatherburn P, Hickson F, Reid D et al (2006) Evaluation of the Department of Health funded fasTe HIV testing in the community pilots. London: Sigma Research. www.sigmaresearch.org.uk/go.php/ projects/project42

28. British Medical Association (2007) The Mental Capacity Act 2005 - Guidance for health professionals. London: British Medical Association. http://www.bma.org.uk/ap.nsf/Content/mencapact0 OpenDocument&Highlight=2,mental,capacity

29. British Medical Association and Law Society (2004) *Assessment of mental capacity: guidance for doctors and lawyers: 2nd edition.* London: BMJ Publications.

30. British Medical Association (2002) *Medical treatment for adults with incapacity: guidance on ethical and medico-legal issues in Scotland.* London: British Medical Association. http://www.bma.org.uk/ ap.nsf/Content/AdultsincapacitySC

31. Department for Constitutional Affairs (2007) *Mental Capacity Act 2005 Code of Practice.* London: TSO. http://www.dca.gov.uk/legal-policy/mental-capacity/mca-cp.pdf

32. Scottish Government (2007) *Revised codes of practice for the Adults with Incapacity Act.* http://www.scotland.gov.uk/Topics/Justice/Civil/awi/revisedcodes

33. Children's HIV Association of UK and Ireland (2007) *HIV testing of children and young people.* http://www.chiva.org.uk/protocols/testing.html

34. Children's HIV Association of UK and Ireland (2007) *Post-exposure prophylaxis (PEP) Guidelines for children exposed to blood-borne viruses.* http://www.chiva.org.uk/protocols/pep.html

35. General Medical Council (2007) *0-18 years: guidance for all doctors.* http://www.gmc-uk.org/guidance/ethical_guidance/children_guidance/index.asp

36. British Association for Sexual Health and HIV Clinical Effectiveness Group (2002) *National guideline on the management of suspected sexually transmitted infections in children and young people.* http://www.bashh.org/documents/41/41.pdf

37. Royal College of Paediatrics and Child Health (2008) *The physical signs of child sexual abuse. An evidence-based review and guidance for best practice.* Sudbury: Lavenham Press.

38. Department of Health (2004) *HIV post-exposure prophylaxis: guidance from the UK Chief Medical Officer's Expert Advisory Group on AIDS.* http://www. dh.gov.uk/en/Publicationsandstatistics/Publications/ PublicationsPolicyAndGuidance/DH_4083638

39. Association of British Insurers (1994) *ABI statement of practice – underwriting life insurance for HIV/AIDS.* www.abi.org.uk/Display/File/Child/197/HIV_ SoBP_1994.doc

40. Association of British Insurers (2004) *Statement of best practice on HIV and insurance.* http://www.abi.org.uk/Display/File/86/HIV_SoBP_ September_2004.doc

41. Terrence Higgins Trust (THT) website section on criminal prosecution. www.tht.org.uk/informationresources/prosecutions/ accessed 23 July 2008.

42. Anderson J, Chalmers J, Nelson M et al (2006) *HIV transmission, the law and the work of the clinical team. A briefing paper.* http://www.bhiva.org/files/file1001327.pdf